EAGER 2 COOK

Cookbook Series

Healthy Recipes for Healthy Living

Vegan

SPARK Publications
Charlotte, North Carolina

Eager 2 Cook™: Healthy Recipes for Healthy Living
Vegan
E2M Chef Connect LLC

Eager 2 Cook™ series by Golden Spoon Holdings, LLC

The E2M program provides suggestions on eating a whole food diet that has successfully helped tens of thousands of members achieve their weight loss goals. Before you start this or any program, consult with your physician to clear if this program is a fit for you, your body, and your health, taking into account allergies, pregnancy, or any other physical condition. The content in this book is intended to be generally informative and not provide medical or nutritional advice, and has not been evaluated by physicians, nutritionists, or the Food and Drug Administration (FDA). The E2M program makes no healing claims and does not guarantee any health or weight loss successes. Resulting meals depend on preparation and ingredients used, and the E2M program or cookbooks make no warranty regarding the outcome of your use of these recipes.

Designed, produced, and published by
SPARK Publications
SPARKpublications.com
Charlotte, North Carolina

Written by: Chef Jennie Casselman and Chef Andres Chaparro

Photography by: Shane Amoroson

Printed in the United States of America

Paperback, December 2023, ISBN: 978-1-953555-51-9
eBook, December 2023, ISBN: 978-1-953555-53-3

Library of Congress Control Number: 2022923357

Dedication

I dedicate this book to all the people who believed in me. With positive support anything is possible, and the people in my life who support my wild ideas give me the fuel to chase my dreams each day. I would not be successful without you. Thank you.

Jeff Witherspoon

Table of
Contents

Vegan Dishes

Vegan Salads

Smoothies

Oats

Dressings

Spice Blends

Sauces

Journals & Checklists

Introduction to
E2M™ Fitness

What is the E2M™ Program?

It is a virtual, eight-week, rapid body transformation program for adults, which consists of workouts, meal plans, cooking classes, mental fitness, and personal coaching. Workouts are designed for all levels and abilities and can be done at home or a gym. Meal plans vary from week to week and are free of supplements, using only whole, nutrient-dense foods. Our meal plans can accommodate any dietary restrictions, including postpartum recovery and vegan. Each member gains access to certified fitness coaches and thousands of other program members who make up our fitness community. Our Fit Family is made up of people across the world from various backgrounds and age demographics, but what we have in common is one goal: to encourage each other to reach our personal best lifestyle and fitness goals. And after the first eight weeks, the program is available for free to maintain progress.

   This isn't about getting "skinny" or "beach ready"; it's about building a healthier lifestyle, living longer, and getting the most out of the body you've been given. This is a lifestyle of health and wellness, and we have the tools to support you in every step of your journey. Whether you want to lose a few pounds, tone up and get stronger, or learn how to sustain a healthier lifestyle with your family, we'd love to help you.

e2mfitness.com

Note to
Members

To my amazing E2M fitness family, we did it!

This cookbook would not be possible without you. It is my sincere hope that this cookbook becomes another tool you can use to maintain your health for years to come. The chefs put lots of time into this and I am excited to see even better results now that you can be a little more creative and still stay on plan. Cooking can be time consuming, but learning to love the process of preparing healthy meals to fuel your body can make cooking your new hobby.

These cookbooks are for us but not only for us, so feel free to recommend the cookbooks to your family and friends because they need to eat healthy too, and they just might end up joining the E2M family. As you improve your health, your life will also improve. JUST KEEP TRYING. Finally, thank you to our amazing chefs Jennie and Andres! They wanted to share some E2M community favorite recipes, and some new ones, in a usable format to make life easier and being healthy more enjoyable. I hope you love what we put together.

Jeff Witherspoon

"It is my goal to help as many people as possible, and I can't wait to help you improve your health, improve your life! I look forward to the chance to be your guide on your journey to your optimal health and fitness."

– JEFF WITHERSPOON

Jeff Witherspoon

Owner, Founder

Jeff Witherspoon's fitness journey began when he was a young athlete at The Citadel in Charleston, South Carolina. Jeff received a full-ride scholarship and worked without ceasing to quickly become a champion track-and-field athlete. He found great joy in bringing home numerous wins for the Bulldogs.

Upon graduation, Jeff began a successful career in the army as a field artillery officer; he has served our country in several overseas tours. While on a deployment, he found fitness as a way to cope with the stresses of combat. He enjoyed not only the way that working out made his body look but also the way that focusing on his health made him feel. Jeff found that "fitness became a place of release and therapy." Fitness enabled him to manage high levels of stress in the military and to handle more stress in a positive way.

Later in his career, Jeff became a certified hand-to-hand combat instructor for the army. This certification and practice introduced him to another form of fitness and discipline that he also enjoyed. This new level of discipline would eventually permeate all areas of his life.

As Jeff began to encourage fellow soldiers and friends to work out and eat healthy, he recognized his passion to help others. Fitness and nutrition became tools he used to help lead other soldiers with PTSD in coping with day-to-day stressors and to assist them in improving their overall health and wellness. This sparked his desire to become a certified personal trainer.

Jeff's passion and business grew as he began to see how his knowledge and motivation were helping others transform their lives. Providing accurate and factual advice to improve others' fitness levels is his main goal. Through all his experiences, he strategically created what is now E2M Fitness, a worldwide fitness program changing lives one day at a time.

e2mfitness.com

Jennie Casselman

Chef & NASM Certified Nutrition Coach

Growing up in a large southern family, Jennie always enjoyed being in the kitchen with her mom. "I was raised in a family who honored dinnertime. My mom would cook from scratch every night, and then we would all sit around the dinner table and talk about our day." Jennie appreciated all the hard work and commitment it took from her parents to be able to maintain this special tradition for their family.

Her passion for nutrition and food didn't become clear until her late twenties when she was diagnosed with melanoma. "It was a very scary time in my life, but I knew that I could make better decisions for my overall health." She started learning about nutrition and holistic health, which led her to culinary school.

Jennie started her career in nutrition and food service after graduating from Johnson & Wales University in Charlotte, North Carolina. She spent over ten years working in the corporate food service management industry. She trained chefs across the country on how to write nutritious menus for clients of all ages from birth to retirement.

With a background in cheer and dance, Jennie has always enjoyed staying active. She continues to stay active now with E2M workouts and enjoys hiking with her husband and twins. Jennie joined the E2M staff as one of the chefs in November 2020 and has enjoyed teaching online cooking classes and being a part of every life that has been transformed by this program. "My heart's desire is to continue to educate others and share how to fuel your body, as well as to emphasize that healthy can be delicious!"

Andres
Chaparro

Chef

Since he was young, Andres has always been involved with cooking. He started his career as an intern for a small bakery in his hometown. This gave him a little taste of the industry, which was all he needed to realize that he wanted to pursue a culinary career. After receiving formal training from Johnson & Wales University in Charlotte, North Carolina, he began working and gaining experience in kitchens from coast to coast. With over thirteen years of experience in the food service industry, he looks forward to bringing healthy cooking back to the main screen.

Andres first joined the E2M program in 2018 as a community member, which started his love of running. At the end of 2020, Andres transitioned to the E2M staff by providing weekly online cooking classes. Andres has enjoyed teaching countless E2M members how to make simple, healthy, and flavorful food.

"Trust the Process™"

– JEFF WITHERSPOON

e2mfitness.com

E2M™ Fitness
Success Stories

The jaw-dropping before and after photos of our clients are a direct result of following the E2M Fitness meal and exercise program.

The meal plan includes the recipes in all of our cookbooks written by the chefs of E2M Fitness.

Learning how to fuel your body with nutrient-dense proteins, vegetables, and healthy fats is the key to transitioning to a healthier lifestyle. With proper nutrition and exercise you can change your lifestyle! Healthy recipes and healthy habits lead to healthy living.

Success stories are shared throughout this cookbook. To learn more about the fitness program, please visit E2Mfitness.com.

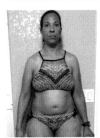     

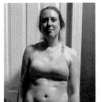 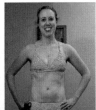 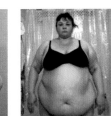 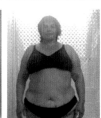  

Meal Prep
Strategy

Why is meal prep so important?

Meal prep has become increasingly popular not only for those with busy schedules but also for those looking to eat healthier. Having healthy options readily available helps to manage cravings and to prevent you from making impulsive choices. Follow some of these time-saving strategies to help ditch the last-minute drive-thru and the extra expense of takeout.

Meal Prep

Meal prep simply means preparing ingredients or whole meals in advance to save you time and set yourself up for success. It can be as simple as washing and chopping vegetables to be ready to cook on those busy weeknights. It can also be cooking and assembling entire meals that can be quickly heated and served for you or your whole family. Chopping vegetables or preparing meal components like your protein will save you time and energy, which we can all use more of during our busy seasons of life. Planned leftovers are another simple strategy to make sure you have healthy choices on hand. When you are preparing one recipe, simply make an extra serving to ensure you have another meal ready to take with you to work the next day. Spending a little extra time in the kitchen once or twice a week preparing your meal components is the key to a successful meal plan strategy.

Meal Prep Containers

Be sure to have plenty of storage containers with airtight lids to maintain quality and freshness. You can use glass or BPA-free plastic containers. For larger batch cooking and freezer meals, foil pans work great. Gallon-size ziplock bags and mason jars are ideal for storage. A vacuum sealer is a great option for preserving large amounts of prepared food, allowing food to remain safe for up to several months in the freezer.

Meal Prep Planning

Choose the recipes you would like to prepare for three to four days of meals. Try to select recipes that use similar ingredients to help reduce your grocery bill. Also check your local grocery store ads and farmers market to buy items that are on sale and seasonally available. You can use the **E2M Weekly Meal Planner** (see checklist pages) to track your recipes and make your grocery list based on your weekly meal plan. Then go to the store!

Grocery Shopping Tips:

1. Print and bring your weekly meal list.

2. Decide on which proteins you would like to prepare.

3. Choose two to three recipes you would like to make and select vegetables and fats to compliment the protein.

4. When shopping, stick to the perimeter of the store. Most of your fresh produce, proteins, and healthy fats are located on the outer perimeter of a grocery store. The inner aisles typically contain prepackaged foods that are not the most nutritious options available. Frozen and canned vegetables are also great options and another great way to meal prep.

5. Dry spices and herbs add loads of flavor to produce and proteins, so be sure to stock your spice cabinet with a variety of spices, including sea salt and black pepper!

6. Double-check food labels and ingredients to make sure there are no added sugars or ingredients that you cannot pronounce!

7. Only buy enough for three to four days so you do not waste food that may spoil quickly, such as fresh meats and produce.

Now you are ready to get in the kitchen and start cooking! Always be sure to read the entire recipe to ensure you are following the steps in order and you have all your ingredients. Enjoy prepping!

Food
Safety

As you embark on your journey and getting back into the kitchen, it is important to know some basic food safety guidelines not only for yourself but also those you will be serving. Food safety plays a big part in your overall health journey. Germs can live in many conditions, so it is important to wash your produce, hands, utensils, and surfaces often while preparing food.

Wash Hands and Surfaces Often

- Never prep raw meat and vegetables on the same cutting board.
- Do not rinse or wash raw meat, seafood, or eggs.
- Did you know that the easiest way to prevent the spread of germs is to properly wash your hands? This is important and needs to be done any time that you are preparing different items in your kitchen. For example, you would need to wash your hands after you touch any uncooked proteins, ready-to-eat items, and vegetables.
- Properly washing your cutting boards with hot, soapy water after preparing each food item and before you go on to the next item is critical. This reduces the spread of germs and the risk of cross contamination.
- Chef Andres and Chef Jennie prefer to use separate cutting boards for proteins and vegetables. Plastic cutting boards are great for meat and wooden is best for vegetables and fruits. Wood boards are porous and can increase the likelihood of cross contamination.

Refrigerate and Store Properly

- As you start this journey into a healthier you, it may be tempting to overshop and pack your refrigerator with healthy items. It is important to not overstock your refrigerator. You need to allow adequate airflow to move throughout and keep the temperature around 40 degrees.
- Refrigerate perishable items like proteins within 2 hours of shopping.
- The freezer will be more efficient if kept full and if the top shelf is not crowded. Just like in the fridge, adequate airflow is critical.
- To prevent cross-contamination, do not store pre-cooked or plant-based "meat" next to raw meat. Wash and rinse all fresh produce before storing it in the fridge.
- Store raw meats and poultry at the bottom of the refrigerator to prevent cross-contamination with produce.

Temperature Control and Reheating

- Did you know there is a safe way to store your prepared meals and reheat them? The most important step of proper storage is not letting the meals stay out at room temperature for a long time before placing them in the refrigerator. When storing the meals in the refrigerator, place the food into smaller 1"-2" deep, airtight containers and ensure the lid is not tightly secured. This will allow steam from the food to escape and adequately cool before placing the lid on and completing this process.
- When reheating your prepared meals, the Centers for Disease Control and Prevention recommends allowing food to reach to 165 degrees. When using a microwave, stir food halfway through cooking.
- By taking these steps, you are heading in the right direction regarding your food safety.

Cooking
Basics

Roasting and Baking
(325 to 450 degrees)

Roasting and baking are similar types of dry-heat cooking methods that use hot air to cook food. Roasting and baking at 325 to 450 degrees will brown the surface of the food, which will enhance the flavor. Roasting is a cooking method that can be done on sheet pans or roasting dishes. Chef Jennie prefers to roast on sheet pans covered with parchment paper to make for easy cleanup.

Roasting and baking are done in a standard oven. This technique cooks food evenly, at the same heat and at the same time. Roasting and baking require food be cooked uncovered to allow hot, dry air to circulate freely around the food. Proteins and vegetables can easily be cooked together with this technique. Be sure not to overcrowd your pan by putting food too close together. You want the air to circulate around the food to give it a nice crispy outside.

A meat thermometer is an extremely helpful tool to figure out the internal temperature of your protein and to know when it is a safe temperature for consuming. Cooking times can vary depending on equipment, so the use of a meat thermometer is the most exact way to find the internal temperature.

Cooking Tip: Prepare food for roasting and baking by cutting it into similar sizes so it cooks evenly.
Cooking Tip: Cover your sheet pan with parchment paper to clean up easily and to preserve the surface of the pans longer.

Broiling
(500 degrees)

Broiling is also a dry-heat cooking method that requires the food to be close to the heat source. This will cook the surface of the food quickly as well as brown the surface for more flavor. Chef Jennie and Chef Andres like to finish off dishes, especially chicken and fish, with two to three minutes under the broiler to enhance the flavors already used for the foods.

Cooking Tip: Stay close by when broiling; it only takes the broiler a few minutes before it can burn your food.

Grilling
(high heat)

Grilling simply means heating the food from below with high heat, whether using a gas, charcoal, or indoor grill. The food is typically only turned one time during the cooking process, giving the food the ever-so-desired grill marks. Grilling can also be achieved with a grill pan or grill grate that goes over a gas stove top. As with most cooking methods, it is important to heat the grill before adding the food and to make sure your grill grates are clean. Rather than oiling the pans or grates as you would with other cooking methods, oil your food directly when grilling.

Fish, chicken, vegetables, and fruit are better off being cooked at a lower temperature on the grill for a longer time.

Safety Tip: Always make sure the tools you use with a grill are specific for grilling and can stand up to high heat.

Sauté
(low to medium heat)

Sautéing is one of the most common ways to cook protein and vegetables at home. It is a quick cooking method that requires a little oil and a wide shallow pan. A helpful tip for sautéing food evenly is to not overcrowd your pan with too much food. Overcrowding can cause the heat to decrease and create steam that would end up steaming your food instead of sautéing it. To sauté food and make sure it cooks evenly, you can toss the food in the pan, then flip or move it around with a spatula. Think *Top Chef* or hibachi chef tricks!

It is important to allow your pan to heat up before adding a small amount of oil that has a high smoke point. Extra-virgin olive oil has a lower smoke point and will burn quickly. Allow the cooking oil to heat for a minute before adding the ingredients to the pan. Chef Jennie's and Chef Andres's recommended cooking oils are avocado oil and coconut oil spray.

Safety Tip: If using spray oils, please do not use over an open flame. Spray the pan prior to turning on a gas stove top.

Steaming and Boiling

Steaming and boiling are both low-fat cooking methods that do not require cooking oil. They do cook food at higher temperatures since the water needs to be boiling, but the indirect heat is what cooks the food during steaming. You will need a deep-sided pot and a steaming basket. Make sure to put enough water in the pot so that it doesn't evaporate out, but not too much to cause it to boil over. Most vegetables are excellent options for food for steaming and boiling.

Cast-Iron Skillet

Stove Top Cooking with Cast Iron: Cast iron's ability to absorb and distribute heat evenly makes it one of the best cooking vessels. Allow the cast-iron skillet to come to temperature by putting it over the heat for five to ten minutes to thoroughly heat. Once it reaches the desired temperature, it can consistently hold that temperature for an extended period of time, allowing you to cook your food evenly.

Chef Andres says, "When it comes to different cuts of meat, the best cooking process is a combination of both high- and low-temperature cooking methods." A cast-iron skillet is the perfect vessel for this method. Elevated temperatures sear and caramelize the outside, giving it the perfect outer crust to your protein. Chef Jennie loves to sear chicken and beef at a high heat to start and then finish off the cooking in the oven. Chef Jennie prefers to use her cast-iron skillet for most cooking methods!

Grilling with Cast Iron: Fish and vegetables can be challenging to grill since they are delicate. Using a cast-iron pan or griddle allows you to get that over-the-fire flavor without losing your food between the grates.

Safety and Care of Cast Iron: Cast-iron skillets require particular care but are worth it and will last for decades! Cleaning cast iron is easy. Avoid harsh detergents and soaps. If food is cooked onto the surface, add water and turn on the heat to bring it to a simmer. Use a wooden spoon to scrape the food from the pan and rinse. Once the skillet is clean and completely dry, rub it with a small amount of high-temperature oil—like avocado oil or coconut oil—to prevent rusting. This last step is the most important, according to Chef Jennie: don't forget to "season" your cast-iron skillet to prevent rust.

Meet the
Certified Trainers

Mandy

"Fitness is
all-or-something,
not all-or-nothing"

Alicia

"Your GOAL is your destination!
Your ACTIONS are your vehicle!
CONSISTENCY and DISCIPLINE
are your fuel! Enjoy the journey
as much as the destination"

Whit

"The body
achieves what
the mind believes"

Suggested
Kitchen Tools

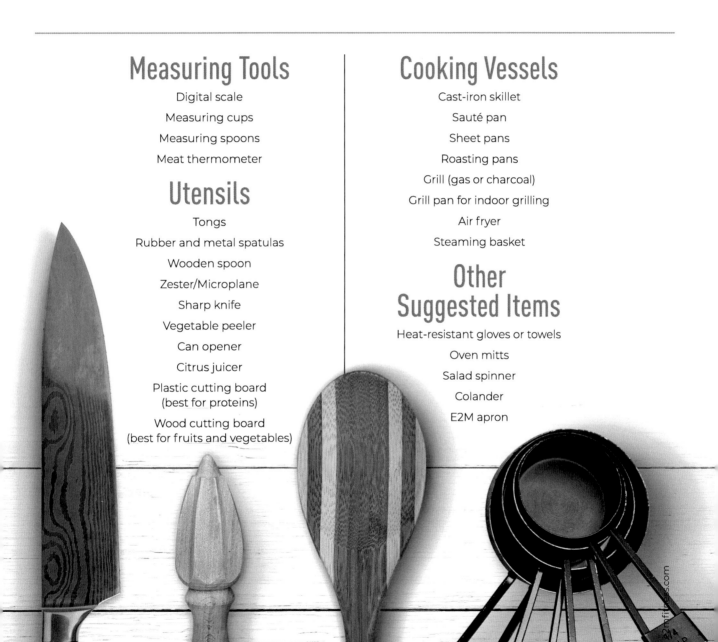

Measuring Tools

Digital scale

Measuring cups

Measuring spoons

Meat thermometer

Utensils

Tongs

Rubber and metal spatulas

Wooden spoon

Zester/Microplane

Sharp knife

Vegetable peeler

Can opener

Citrus juicer

Plastic cutting board
(best for proteins)

Wood cutting board
(best for fruits and vegetables)

Cooking Vessels

Cast-iron skillet

Sauté pan

Sheet pans

Roasting pans

Grill (gas or charcoal)

Grill pan for indoor grilling

Air fryer

Steaming basket

Other
Suggested Items

Heat-resistant gloves or towels

Oven mitts

Salad spinner

Colander

E2M apron

How to
Work with Tofu

Tofu is a versatile vegan protein option and can be used in many ways. When cooking with tofu, it's important to first remove the excess water. Remove the tofu from its package, and put the tofu block between several layers of paper towels. Place something heavy on top to press down on the tofu; this will help remove the excess moisture, allowing the tofu to sauté instead of steam. You may also use a tofu press, which is another great way to remove the excess water. Tofu is like a sponge; it does not have much flavor on its own, but it will soak up all the herbs and spices that you use. Allowing the tofu additional time to marinate further imparts the flavor.

Vegan Dishes

Tarragon Tofu
with Vegetables

PREP
30
MINUTES

COOK
20
MINUTES

SERVES
4

Ingredients

- 2 (14-ounce) packages extra-firm tofu
- 1 lemon, zested and juiced
- ¼ cup olive oil
- 1 tablespoon minced garlic
- 2 teaspoons sea salt
- ½ teaspoon black pepper
- 1 (1-ounce) package fresh tarragon leaves, rough chopped
- 6 cups sliced bell peppers (red, yellow, or green)
- 2 (14-ounce) cans artichoke hearts, drained and quartered

Prep

1. Drain and press the tofu, then cut into 1-inch cubes.

2. Make the marinade in a large bowl by combining the lemon zest, lemon juice, olive oil, garlic, sea salt, and black pepper; mix well. Add half of the chopped fresh tarragon, reserving the rest for garnish. Add the tofu, bell peppers, and artichoke hearts to the bowl; toss to coat. Marinate for 30 minutes or longer in the refrigerator. When the tofu is almost done marinating, preheat the oven to 450 degrees. Line a sheet pan with parchment paper.

Cook

3. Spread out the marinated tofu and vegetables on the sheet pan. Bake for 15 minutes, then broil for 2 to 3 minutes to brown.

Serve

4. Plate tofu and vegetables, and garnish with the reserved fresh tarragon.

Veggie Tofu
Scramble

PREP
10
MINUTES

COOK
10
MINUTES

SERVES
4

Ingredients

- 2 (14-ounce) packages firm tofu
- Cooking oil spray
- 2 cups kale
- 2 cups cauliflower rice
- 1 cup seeded and diced red bell peppers
- 1 zucchini, diced
- 1 tablespoon chopped black olives
- 1 teaspoon sea salt
- ¼ teaspoon ground turmeric
- ½ teaspoon black pepper

Prep

1. Drain and press the tofu. Chop the tofu, then use a fork to crumble it into bite-size pieces. Add sea salt, pepper, and turmeric. Set aside.

Cook

2. Heat a large frying pan over medium-high heat; spray with cooking oil. Add the kale, cauliflower rice, red bell peppers, zucchini, and black olives to the hot pan; sauté for 3 minutes. Add the crumbled tofu; stir until well combined. Continue to cook for 5 to 10 minutes, stirring occasionally.

Serve

3. Divide the scrambled tofu between bowls.

Thai Vegan Beef
Stir-Fry

Ingredients

Vegan Beef:

- Cooking oil spray
- 1 pound ground vegan beef or crumbles
- 2 green onions, chopped
- 1 teaspoon ground garlic
- 1 teaspoon sea salt
- 1 teaspoon sesame oil
- ½ teaspoon ground ginger
- ½ teaspoon crushed red pepper
- ¼ cup water

Stir-Fry Base:

- 4 cups thinly sliced red cabbage
- 1 cup thinly sliced celery
- 1 cup grated carrots
- 1 cup diced red bell peppers
- 1 lime, zested and juiced
- 1 cup chopped peanuts
- Chopped cilantro (for garnish)

PREP
10
MINUTES

COOK
15
MINUTES

SERVES
4

Prep

1. Heat a skillet over medium heat; spray with cooking oil.

Cook

2. Add the vegan beef, breaking it up into smaller pieces in the pan. Add the chopped green onions, garlic, sea salt, sesame oil, ginger, crushed red pepper, and water; mix well. Continue cooking until the vegan beef is cooked through, or reaches an internal temperature of 165 degrees, 8 to 12 minutes. Remove from the pan.

3. In the same pan, squeeze the juice from ½ lime and stir to remove cooked-on food from the bottom. Add the cabbage, celery, carrots, and red bell peppers. Sauté for 5 to 7 minutes, until tender.

Serve

4. Plate the vegetable stir-fry. Top with vegan beef and chopped peanuts; garnish with cilantro and remaining lime juice and zest.

E2M Success Stories

Antoine B., Gainesville Fl

 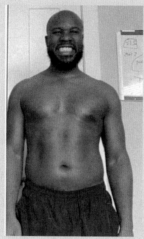

Rounds	Age	Weight Loss
1	40	20

Initially, to be honest, I wanted to win the prize money. Instead, we gained so much more! I've made physical exercise part of my daily routine. My wife says my stamina has greatly improved. And losing weight makes me like how I look in my clothes.

What did you want to change about your lifestyle?
I wanted to change the lack of energy that I had.

What does the E2M fitness community mean to you?
It means having a community of friends all striving to help each other become healthier.

Bernadette DD., Advance, NC

Rounds	Age	Weight Loss
6	46	33

I could not exercise without pain. I did not have the discipline to fuel my body with the right foods. Now that I have been with E2M fitness for a year, I am running better than I did in my 20s. I eat plant based to maintain my heart health and I now know how to help my family stay healthy too.

Non-Scale Victory (NSV)!
I got my high 151 LDL cholesterol down to optimum at 106. All of my labs are now normal. I decreased my dose of beta blocker and I'm training to run a marathon.

e2mfitness.com

Korean Edamame
Bowl

Ingredients

Base:

- 4 cups edamame
- ½ teaspoon ground garlic
- ½ teaspoon onion powder
- ¼ teaspoon ground ginger
- ¼ teaspoon sea salt

- ⅛ teaspoon crushed red pepper
- Cooking oil spray
- 1 lime, zested and juiced
- 4 cups cauliflower rice, frozen or fresh, prepared

Toppings:

- 1 cucumber, thinly sliced
- 2 avocados, peeled and diced

- ½ red onion, diced small
- ½ teaspoon sesame seeds

Cook

1. Heat a large pan over medium-high heat; spray with cooking oil. Add the edamame. Add the garlic, onion powder, ginger, sea salt, and crushed red pepper; mix thoroughly. Cook until edamame is tender and seasoned. Remove from pan.

2. Turn the heat down to medium. Squeeze the juice from ½ lime into the pan. Add the cauliflower rice; sauté for 5 to 8 minutes.

Serve

3. Divide the cauliflower rice between bowls, and top with the edamame; add the prepared cucumber, avocado, and red onion. Garnish with sesame seeds and the zest and juice from the remaining 1/2-1 cup lime.

PREP
10
MINUTES

COOK
15
MINUTES

SERVES
4

Tempeh Taco
Salad

PREP
10
MINUTES

COOK
15
MINUTES

SERVES
4

Ingredients

Protein:
- Cooking oil spray
- 1 pound diced tempeh
- ½ cup thinly sliced mushrooms
- 1 teaspoon ground garlic
- 1 teaspoon chili powder
- 1 tablespoon smoked paprika
- ½ teaspoon ground cumin
- ¼ teaspoon sea salt
- ⅛ teaspoon black pepper

Salad:
- 4 cups spring mix
- 4 cups chopped romaine lettuce
- ½ cup grated carrots
- 2 avocados, peeled and diced
- 1 cup sliced cucumbers
- ½ cup thinly sliced green onions
- ½ cup thinly sliced red bell peppers

Prep

1. Heat a skillet to medium heat and spray with cooking oil. Add the diced tempeh.

Cook

2. Add the tempeh and mushrooms; cook for 6 to 8 minutes, until golden brown.

3. Add the garlic, chili powder, smoked paprika, cumin, sea salt, and black pepper; stir and cook for another 5 minutes, until all the seasonings are well distributed and the tempeh is browned. Remove the pan from the heat.

Serve

4. In a large bowl, toss the spring mix and romaine; add the carrots, avocado, cucumbers, green onions, red bell peppers, and ½-1 cup tempeh.

Note:
This salad pairs well with the Avocado Lime Dressing.

Chimichurri Tofu
Lettuce Tacos

**PREP
30
MINUTES**

**COOK
20
MINUTES**

**SERVES
4**

Ingredients

Protein:

- 2 (14-ounce) packages extra-firm tofu
- Cooking oil spray
- 2 red or green bell peppers, seeded and thinly sliced
- ½ red onion, thinly sliced
- Lettuce leaves (Bibb or romaine)
- 2 avocados, peeled and diced
- Chimichurri Sauce (see page 128)

Prep

1. Drain and press the tofu, then cut into ½-inch cubes.

2. For the Chimichurri Sauce, combine the ingredients in a food processor, and blend until smooth. Reserve 3 tablespoons of sauce. Transfer the remaining Chimichurri Sauce to a large bowl, add the cubed tofu, and toss to coat evenly. Marinate in the refrigerator for at least 30 minutes.

Cook

3. Heat a pan over medium heat; spray with cooking oil. Add the marinated tofu and sauté in batches over medium heat until the tofu is lightly golden, 2 to 3 minutes on each side. Note that it is best to cook the tofu in batches. Set aside the tofu. Add the bell peppers and red onions to the pan; sauté for 3 to 5 minutes, or until tender.

Serve

4. Place a large lettuce leaf on each plate; put the tofu with the sautéed onions and peppers on the lettuce; top with diced avocado and the reserved Chimichurri Sauce.

Meal prep idea:

Store the tofu and vegetables together in an airtight container; put the lettuce leaves in a ziplock bag with a paper towel. Refrigerate for up to three days. Assemble when ready to eat.

Greek Vegan
Beef Bowl

Ingredients

Vegetables:
- 1 (14-ounce) can artichokes, drained and quartered
- 1 cup sliced black olives
- 1 cup diced English cucumber
- 1 cup diced red bell peppers
- 1 tablespoon olive oil
- 1 lemon, juiced
- ¼ teaspoon sea salt
- ⅛ teaspoon black pepper

Vegan Beef:
- Cooking oil spray
- 2 tablespoons spice blend (recipe below)
- 2 pounds ground vegan beef
- Fresh parsley (for garnish)

Spice Blend:
- 2 teaspoons ground garlic
- ½ teaspoon sea salt
- 2 teaspoons dried rosemary
- 2 teaspoons dried oregano
- ½ teaspoon black pepper
- ½ teaspoon lemon zest

Prep

1. Combine all the ingredients for the spice blend; mix thoroughly.

2. Combine the artichokes, black olives, cucumber, and red bell peppers. Add the olive oil, juice of one lemon, sea salt, and black pepper; toss to combine.

Cook

3. Heat a large pan or cast-iron skillet over medium heat; spray with cooking oil. Add 2 tablespoons of the spice blend and stir until fragrant, about 30 seconds. Add the vegan beef, breaking it up into smaller pieces in the pan; cook and stir until browned.

Serve

4. Divide the vegetable mixture between bowls, and top with the vegan beef; garnish with fresh parsley.

Spicy Green Harissa
Tofu Salad

PREP
35
MINUTES

COOK
35
MINUTES

SERVES
4

Note:
This salad pairs well with the Thai Peanut Dressing.

Ingredients

- 2 (14-ounce) packages extra-firm tofu
- 6 cups spring mix
- 1 tablespoon chopped green onions
- 2 cups thinly sliced cucumber
- 2 cups shredded carrots
- 1 tablespoon chopped fresh cilantro
- Spicy Green Harrisa sauce (see page 129)
- 2 tablespoons rice vinegar
- 1 tablespoon olive oil
- 1 tablespoon smoked paprika
- 1 teaspoon ground garlic
- 1 teaspoon ground ginger

Prep

1. Drain the tofu, then cut into 1-inch cubes. Prepare the Spicy Green Harissa sauce and set aside.

2. In a medium bowl, toss the tofu cubes with the rice vinegar, paprika, ginger, and garlic. Marinate for 30 minutes or longer in the refrigerator. When the tofu is almost done marinating, preheat the oven to 400 degrees. Line a sheet pan with parchment paper or spray with cooking oil.

Cook

3. Spread out the marinated tofu on the pan. Bake for 30 to 35 minutes; flip the tofu halfway through. Cool and sprinkle with Everything but the Bagel seasoning or sesame seeds.
   Air fryer option: Cook at 400 degrees for 15 minutes.

Serve

4. Plate the spring mix with the baked tofu; top with green onions, cucumber, and shredded carrots. Garnish with fresh cilantro.

Thai Tofu
Stir-Fry Bowl

Ingredients

Tofu:

- 2 (14-ounce) packages extra-firm tofu
- 2 cups shredded cabbage or slaw
- 1 cucumber, diced
- 1 cup chopped peanuts
- ¼ cup chopped fresh cilantro
- 2 tablespoons sesame seeds
- 1 lime, zested and juiced

Stir-Fry Marinade:

- 2 tablespoons rice vinegar
- 1 tablespoon olive oil
- 1 tablespoon chili powder
- 1 teaspoon ground garlic
- ¼ teaspoon ground ginger
- ½ lime, zested and juiced
- 1 ½ teaspoons sea salt
- Crushed red pepper (optional)
- Hot sauce (optional)

PREP
30
MINUTES

COOK
25
MINUTES

SERVES
4

Prep

1. Drain and press the tofu, then chop into medium dice.

2. Make the stir-fry marinade in a medium bowl by whisking together the rice vinegar, olive oil, chili powder, garlic, ginger, lime zest, sea salt, and lime juice, including any optional crushed red pepper or hot sauce. Add the diced tofu to the sauce; toss to coat evenly. Marinate for 30 minutes or longer in the refrigerator.

Cook

3. Heat a cast-iron skillet or sauté pan over medium heat; spray with cooking oil. Add the marinated tofu and sauté for 15 to 20 minutes, until browned.

4. Before the tofu is finished cooking, heat a separate pan over medium heat; spray with cooking oil. Combine the shredded cabbage with 2 tablespoons of the stir-fry marinade, and sauté for 5 minutes to soften.

Serve

5. Divide the shredded cabbage, tofu, cucumber, and peanuts between bowls. Top with chopped cilantro, sesame seeds, lime juice, and lime zest.

Cilantro Lime
Tofu Bowl

PREP
35
MINUTES

COOK
35
MINUTES

SERVES
4

Ingredients

Tofu:
- 2 (14-ounce) packages extra-firm tofu
- 2 tablespoons olive oil
- ½ teaspoon ground cumin
- ½ teaspoon chili powder
- ½ teaspoon ground garlic
- 1 teaspoon paprika
- 2 limes, zested and juiced
- Sesame seeds or Everything but the Bagel seasoning

Avocado Salsa:
- 2 avocados, peeled and diced
- 1 lime, juiced
- 2 tablespoons chopped fresh cilantro

Cauliflower Rice:
- 4 cups cauliflower rice, fresh or frozen
- ¼ cup chopped cilantro
- ½ lime, zested and juiced
- 1 teaspoon sea salt
- ¼ teaspoon black pepper

Prep

1. Drain and press the tofu, then cut into 1-inch cubes.

2. In a medium bowl, combine the olive oil, cumin, chili powder, garlic, paprika, lime zest, and lime juice. Add the tofu cubes and toss to coat evenly in the marinade. Marinate for 30 minutes or longer in the refrigerator.

3. To make the avocado salsa, combine the avocado, lime juice, and chopped cilantro. Toss to combine. Cover and refrigerate if not using immediately.

4. When the tofu is almost done marinating, preheat the oven to 400 degrees. Line a sheet pan with parchment paper or spray with cooking oil. Spread out the marinated tofu on the pan.

Cook

5. Bake for 30 to 35 minutes, flipping the tofu halfway through. Allow to cool, and sprinkle with sesame seeds or Everything but the Bagel seasoning.
   Air fryer option: Cook at 400 degrees for 15 minutes.

6. Heat a skillet to medium heat; spray with cooking oil. Sauté the cauliflower rice for 5 minutes and remove from the heat. After the cauliflower has cooled, puree the cauliflower if preferred or leave as is. Add chopped cilantro and the zest and juice of ½ lime.

Serve

7. Divide the cauliflower between bowls; top with the tofu and avocado salsa.

Vegan Sausage
with Roasted Peppers

PREP
10
MINUTES

COOK
20
MINUTES

SERVES
4

Ingredients

Roasted Peppers and Vegan Sausage:

- 2 red bell peppers, seeded and sliced
- 2 green bell peppers, seeded and sliced
- 1 yellow bell pepper, seeded and sliced
- 2 tablespoons olive oil
- 2 teaspoons sea salt
- 1 teaspoon ground garlic
- 1 teaspoon smoked paprika
- 1 teaspoon ground cumin
- 1 teaspoon black pepper
- 2 (14-ounce) packages vegan Italian sausage links

Mashed Cauliflower:

- 1 tablespoon olive oil
- ½ cup diced sweet onions
- 2 garlic cloves, minced
- 1 cup water
- 2 (12-ounce) bags cauliflower rice (frozen or shelf stable)
- 1 teaspoon sea salt
- 1 teaspoon black pepper

Prep

1. Preheat the oven to 375 degrees. Line a sheet pan with parchment paper.

2. In a large bowl, combine the red, green, and yellow bell peppers with the olive oil, sea salt, garlic, smoked paprika, cumin, and black pepper; toss to mix thoroughly. Spread out the peppers on the prepared sheet pan; put the vegan sausage links on top, evenly spread across the peppers.

Cook

3. Bake the peppers and vegan sausage for 10 to 15 minutes, until the sausage is fully cooked and reaches an internal temperature of 165 degrees.

4. While the peppers and sausage are baking, heat 1 tablespoon olive oil in a large pot over medium heat. Add the onions and garlic; cook until the onions are softened, 2 to 4 minutes. Add the cauliflower rice, water, sea salt, and black pepper; cook for 5 minutes or until tender and most of the water has been cooked out. Blend with an immersion blender; be mindful while using an immersion blender with hot food, as it can splatter.

Serve

5. Plate the pureed cauliflower, sautéed peppers, and 2 vegan sausages per serving.

Vegan Beef
Burrito Bowl

Ingredients

Vegetables:

- 2 avocados, peeled and sliced
- 1½ limes, zested and juiced, divided
- 1½ cups diced bell peppers (any color)
- 1 cup sliced red onions
- 1½ teaspoons chopped fresh cilantro (for garnish)

Vegan Beef:

- 2 tablespoons Chili-Lime Seasoning (see page 118)
- 2 pounds ground vegan beef
- Cooking oil spray

Cauliflower Rice:

- 4 cups cauliflower rice, frozen or fresh, prepared
- 1½ teaspoons chopped fresh cilantro
- ¼ teaspoon sea salt
- ⅛ teaspoon black pepper
- ½ lime, zested and juiced

PREP
15
MINUTES

COOK
25
MINUTES

SERVES
4

Prep

1. Combine the ingredients for the Chili-Lime Seasoning and mix well.
2. Mash the avocado slices with the zest and juice of 1 lime.

Cook

3. Heat a large pan or cast-iron skillet over medium heat; spray with cooking oil. Add the Chili-Lime Seasoning and stir until fragrant, about 30 seconds. Add the ground vegan beef; cook and stir until browned. Remove the meat from the skillet.

4. In the same pan over medium heat, squeeze the juice from ½ lime and scrape the pan to remove any cooked-on meat. Add the bell peppers and red onions; sauté until tender.

5. Prepare the cauliflower rice with fresh cilantro, sea salt, black pepper, and the zest and juice of ½ lime.

Serve

6. Layer each burrito bowl with cauliflower rice as the base, then top with the vegetable mixture and vegan beef; garnish with fresh cilantro and mashed avocado.

Curry Lentils
over Cauliflower Rice

PREP
5
MINUTES

COOK
45
MINUTES

SERVES
4

Ingredients

Lentils:
- Curry Powder spice blend (see page 125)
- 2 cups lentils
- 1 tablespoon olive oil
- ½ cup diced onions
- 1½ teaspoons minced garlic

- 6 cups water
- ½ cup tahini
- 4 cups spinach
- 1 lime, zested and juiced
- 2 tablespoons chopped fresh cilantro

Cauliflower Rice:
- Cooking oil spray
- 2 (12-ounce) bags cauliflower rice, frozen or shelf stable

- ¼ teaspoon sea salt
- ¼ teaspoon black pepper
- 1 lime, zested and juiced

Prep

1. For the curry spice blend, combine the ingredients and set aside. Rinse lentils under cold water until the water runs clear.

Cook

2. Heat the olive oil in a large deep nonstick skillet over medium heat. Add the onions and garlic; sauté for about 3 minutes until tender. Add in 2-3 tablespoons of the curry spice blend; sauté for 1 to 2 minutes until fragrant. Slowly add in the water; stir to combine, making a broth.

3. Stir in the rinsed lentils. Reduce the heat to low and cover; simmer for 25 to 30 minutes, or until the lentils are cooked through and mostly softened. If the lentils are not soft, add another ½ cup water and cook for an additional 5 minutes.

4. Turn off the heat and remove the lid; stir in the tahini paste. Allow to sit for 5 to 10 minutes to thicken and cool; fold in the spinach, allowing it to wilt slightly. Add the zest and juice of 1 lime.

5. To make the cauliflower rice, heat a separate pan over medium heat; spray with cooking oil. Add the cauliflower rice, sea salt, black pepper, and zest and juice of the other lime; cook for 3 to 4 minutes, until the cauliflower is heated and fully cooked.

Serve

6. Divide the cauliflower rice between bowls; top with the curry lentils. Garnish with fresh cilantro.

Chimichurri Chickpea
and Cauliflower Tacos

Ingredients

Vegetable Mixture:

- 5 cups chickpeas, drained and rinsed
- Taco seasoning (recipe below)
- 4 cups chopped cauliflower
- 1 tablespoon olive oil
- Cooking oil spray
- ½ cup diced red onions
- 1 lime, zested and juiced
- 1 tablespoon chopped fresh cilantro

Taco Seasoning:

- 1 tablespoon chili powder
- 1 teaspoon ground cumin
- 1 teaspoon sea salt
- ½ teaspoon cayenne pepper
- ½ teaspoon ground garlic

Toppings:

- ¼ cup Chimichurri Sauce (see page 128)
- Lettuce leaves (Bibb or iceberg)
- 2 avocados, peeled and diced
- 1 jalapeño, seeded and diced
- 1 lime, cut into wedges (optional garnish)
- 1 bunch fresh cilantro, chopped (optional garnish)

PREP
5
MINUTES

COOK
20
MINUTES

SERVES
4

Prep

1. Drain and rinse the chickpeas. Set aside on a kitchen towel and dry; this will allow the chickpeas to get crispy. Prepare the Chimichurri Sauce and set aside. Store extra in an airtight container and refrigerate for up to five days.

2. For the taco seasoning, whisk together all the ingredients in a small bowl. In a large bowl, toss the chickpeas and cauliflower with olive oil. Add in the taco seasoning; toss to combine.

Cook

3. Heat a large skillet over medium heat; spray with cooking oil. Add the red onions; sauté for 3 minutes, or until tender. Cook the chickpea mixture in batches, if necessary, to allow enough room in the pan so the chickpeas get crispy instead of letting them steam. Sauté each batch for 8 to 10 minutes. Remove from the heat. Stir in the zest and juice of 1 lime and 1 tablespoon fresh cilantro.

Serve

4. Plate the lettuce leaves; spoon the vegetable mixture into the center of each leaf. Top with diced avocado, jalapeño, and Chimichurri Sauce. Garnish with lime wedges and more fresh cilantro, if desired.

Buffalo Tofu
Nuggets

PREP
30
MINUTES

COOK
30
MINUTES

SERVES
4

Ingredients

Tofu Nuggets:
- 2 (14-ounce) packages extra-firm tofu
- 4 cups spring mix
- Celery (optional for serving)
- Carrots (optional for serving)

Buffalo Sauce:
- ½ teaspoon ground garlic
- ½ teaspoon onion powder
- ½ teaspoon paprika
- 1 teaspoon chili powder
- 1 tablespoon Dijon mustard
- 1½ teaspoons apple cider vinegar
- 1 tablespoon water
- Ground cayenne pepper (optional)

Prep

1. Drain the tofu, then chop into medium dice or cut into triangles.

2. In a medium bowl, whisk together all the ingredients for the buffalo sauce. Add the tofu; toss to coat evenly. Marinate for 30 minutes or longer in the refrigerator. If using the oven option for baking, preheat the oven to 400 degrees and line a sheet pan with parchment paper.

Cook

3. Heat a cast-iron skillet or sauté pan over medium-high heat; spray with cooking oil. Add the marinated tofu, and sauté for 2 to 3 minutes on each side until browned.

4. Transfer to the sheet pan and bake for 30 to 35 minutes.
   Air fryer option: Transfer to an air fryer and cook at 400 degrees for 15 minutes.

Serve

5. Plate the spring mix, and top with buffalo nuggets. Serve with celery or carrots, if desired.

Pineapple Chickpea
Fried Cauliflower Rice

PREP
5
MINUTES

COOK
20
MINUTES

SERVES
4

Ingredients

Vegetables:

- 4 cups chickpeas, drained and rinsed
- Cooking oil spray
- 1 tablespoon minced garlic

- ½ teaspoon ground ginger
- 1 cup shredded carrots
- ½ cup diced yellow onions
- 1 red bell pepper, thinly sliced

Cauliflower Rice:

- 2 limes, zested and juiced
- 1 cup diced pineapple, fresh or canned (drained)
- 4 cups cauliflower rice

- 1 cup cashews
- 1 tablespoon chopped fresh cilantro

Prep

1. Drain and rinse the chickpeas. Set aside on a kitchen towel and dry.

Cook

2. Heat a large skillet over medium heat; spray with cooking oil. Add the garlic and ginger; sauté for 2 to 3 minutes until fragrant. Add the chickpeas, carrots, onions, and bell pepper; sauté for 8 to 10 minutes or until tender. Transfer the vegetables to a heat-resistant bowl.

3. To prepare the cauliflower rice, squeeze the juice of 1 lime into the same pan; use a wooden spoon to scrape any food left on the bottom. Add in the pineapple, cauliflower rice, and zest of 1 lime; sauté for 3 minutes. Once the cauliflower rice is heated through, return the vegetable mixture to the pan and stir to combine.

Serve

4. Plate the cauliflower rice mixture; top with cashews, fresh cilantro, and juice of the other lime.

Roasted Italian
Chickpeas

Ingredients

Tofu and Vegetables:
- 4 cups chickpeas, drained and rinsed
- 2 cups thinly sliced red bell peppers
- 2 cups thinly sliced zucchini
- 1 cup thinly sliced red onions
- 1 cup sliced black olives

Italian Vinaigrette:
- ¼ cup extra-virgin olive oil
- ¼ cup red wine vinegar
- ¼ teaspoon dried parsley
- ¼ teaspoon dried oregano
- ⅛ teaspoon ground garlic
- ⅛ teaspoon crushed red pepper
- Sea salt, to taste
- Black pepper, to taste

PREP 35 MINUTES

Prep

1. For the Italian vinaigrette, combine all the ingredients in a mason jar, secure the lid, and shake.

2. In a medium bowl, toss the chickpeas with the Italian vinaigrette to coat evenly. Marinate for 30 minutes or longer in the refrigerator.

3. Preheat the oven to 400 degrees. Line a sheet pan with parchment paper or spray with cooking oil. Spread out the chickpeas on the pan. Toss the red bell peppers, zucchini, and red onions in the remaining dressing; add to the sheet pan.

COOK 35 MINUTES

Cook

4. Bake for 30 to 35 minutes, flipping halfway through.
   Air fryer option: Cook at 400 degrees for 10 minutes.

SERVES 4

Serve

5. Plate the chickpeas with the vegetables, and top with black olives.

Buffalo Chickpea
Cauliflower

PREP
20
MINUTES

COOK
17
MINUTES

SERVES
4

Ingredients

Cauliflower:

- 2 heads fresh cauliflower
- 4 cups chickpeas, drained and rinsed
- 2 tablespoons olive oil
- 2 teaspoons ground garlic
- 2 tablespoons paprika
- 1 tablespoon chili powder
- ⅛ teaspoon sea salt
- ⅛ teaspoon black pepper
- Sliced celery (for garnish)
- Sliced carrots (for garnish)

Hot sauce:

- 3 tablespoons hot sauce (milder green or hotter red sauce)
- 1 tablespoon water
- 2 teaspoons apple cider vinegar
- Ground cayenne or crushed red pepper (optional)

Prep

1. Preheat the oven to 425 degrees. Line a baking sheet with parchment paper. Cut up the fresh cauliflower into bite-size pieces. Drain and rinse chickpeas.

2. In a bowl, mix the garlic, paprika, chili powder, sea salt, and black pepper. Add the cauliflower and chickpeas. Toss with the spice mix to coat evenly; spread over the prepared baking sheet.

3. Prepare the hot sauce in a large heat-resistant bowl by combining the hot sauce, water, apple cider vinegar, and optional cayenne or crushed red pepper if more heat is desired.

Cook

4. Bake for 15 minutes. Remove the pan and set the oven to broil. Carefully transfer the cauliflower and chickpeas to the bowl with the hot sauce mixture; toss to coat evenly. Return the cauliflower to the pan; broil for 2 minutes.
   Air fryer option: Cook at 350 degrees for 10 minutes.

Serve

5. Serve on a platter garnished with fresh celery and carrots. Enjoy these delicious and easy Buffalo Cauliflower Bites as a healthier twist on wings!

Vegan Tofu
Masala

PREP
20
MINUTES

COOK
20
MINUTES

SERVES
4

Ingredients

Spiced Tofu:
- 2 (14-ounce) packages extra-firm tofu
- 2 tablespoons chopped green onions
- 2 tablespoons chopped cilantro
- Tikka Masala Sauce (see page 129)

Vegetables:
- ¼ cup cashew butter
- 1 cup water
- 1 zucchini
- 1 tablespoon olive oil
- 1 tablespoon chopped garlic cloves
- 1 tablespoon chopped fresh ginger
- 1½ tablespoons Curry Powder spice blend (see page 125)
- 1 green bell pepper, medium diced
- 1 cup chopped green beans
- 4 cups chopped bok choy
- ½ jalapeño, seeded and diced (optional)

Prep

1. Drain the tofu, then cut into 1-inch cubes.

2. To prepare the spice blend, mix all the ingredients together and set aside.

3. In a large bowl, combine the tofu with the Tikka Masala Sauce; mix well. Preheat the oven to 400 degrees. Line a baking pan with parchment paper.

4. Mix the cashew butter and water; set aside. Cut the zucchini in half lengthwise, then slice into 1-inch-thick pieces.

Cook

5. Heat 1 tablespoon olive oil in a large pot or dutch oven over medium heat. Add the garlic and ginger; reduce to low heat to prevent burning. Stir frequently until fragrant and golden, about 2 minutes. Add 1½ tablespoons spice blend and lightly toast while stirring, 1 to 2 minutes.

6. Add the bell peppers, zucchini, green beans, bok choy, and optional jalapeño; stir to mix thoroughly with the spice mixture. Add the prepared cashew butter and water mixture to the pot; cover and simmer for 10 to 12 minutes over medium-low heat. Once the vegetables are done, taste and adjust seasoning if necessary.

7. While the vegetables are simmering, spread the spiced tofu on the parchment-lined baking pan; bake for 10 minutes, or until golden brown.

Serve

8. Plate the vegetables and top with tofu. Garnish with green onions and cilantro.

Spicy Chickpeas
over Cauliflower Rice

Ingredients

Chickpeas:
- 2 tablespoons olive oil
- ½ cup diced red onions
- 2 celery stalks, diced
- 3 garlic cloves, minced
- 1 teaspoon ginger
- 2 cups spinach
- 2 (15-ounce) cans chickpeas, drained, rinsed
- ½ cup creamy peanut butter
- ½ cup water
- 2 tablespoons lemon juice

Spice Blend:
- 2 teaspoons ground coriander
- 1 teaspoon sea salt
- 1 tablespoon smoked paprika
- 1 teaspoon chili powder
- ½ teaspoon crushed red pepper
- ½ teaspoon black pepper
- ½ teaspoon ground turmeric
- Cayenne pepper (optional)

Cauliflower Rice:
- 1 tablespoon olive oil
- 2 (12-ounce) bags cauliflower rice (frozen or shelf stable)
- ¼ teaspoon sea salt
- ¼ teaspoon black pepper

PREP
5
MINUTES

COOK
30
MINUTES

SERVES
4

Prep

1. Prepare the spice blend by combining the coriander, sea salt, smoked paprika, chili powder, crushed red pepper, black pepper, and turmeric.

Cook

2. Heat 2 tablespoons olive oil in a large nonstick skillet over medium heat. Add the red onions and sauté until tender, about 3 minutes. Add the celery, minced garlic, ginger, and spinach; sauté for another 5 minutes. Then add the chickpeas and the prepared spice blend; stir until thoroughly combined. Add the peanut butter, water, and lemon juice; reduce to low heat and cook for another 5 minutes, stirring frequently.

3. For the cauliflower rice, heat 1 tablespoon olive oil in a nonstick skillet over medium heat. Add the cauliflower rice; cook for 3 to 4 minutes, until the cauliflower is heated and fully cooked. Season with sea salt and black pepper.

Serve

4. Divide the cauliflower rice between bowls, and top with the spicy chickpeas.

Vegan
Salads

Jerk Tempeh
Salad

PREP
10
MINUTES

COOK
15
MINUTES

SERVES
4

Ingredients

Tempeh:

- 1 pound tempeh, cut into 1-inch cubes
- 1 tablespoon olive oil
- 1½ tablespoons Jerk Seasoning (see page 119)
- Cooking oil spray

Salad Base:

- 8 cups chopped spring mix
- 1 cup thinly sliced red onions
- 1 cup thinly sliced bell peppers
- 1 cup grated carrots
- 2 avocados, peeled and diced
- 1 cup diced cucumber

Jerk Seasoning:

- 1 tablespoon ground garlic
- 2 teaspoons ground cayenne pepper
- 2 teaspoons onion powder
- 2 teaspoons dried thyme
- 2 teaspoons dried parsley
- 2 teaspoons sea salt
- 1 teaspoon paprika
- 1 teaspoon ground allspice
- ½ teaspoon black pepper
- ½ teaspoon crushed red pepper
- ½ teaspoon ground nutmeg
- ¼ teaspoon ground cinnamon

Prep

1. For the Jerk Seasoning, combine all the ingredients and mix well; store in an airtight container.
2. Combine the tempeh, 1 tablespoon olive oil, and 1½ tablespoons of the Jerk Seasoning; toss to coat evenly.

Cook

3. Heat a skillet over medium-high heat; spray with cooking oil. Add the seasoned tempeh; sauté the tempeh for 3 to 4 minutes, stirring frequently to prevent burning.

Serve

4. To assemble the salad, put the spring mix in a large bowl, and top with arranged rows of the prepared red onions, bell peppers, tempeh, carrots, avocado, and cucumber.

Note:
This salad pairs well with the Cilantro Lime Dressing.

Chopped Autumn Salad
with Vegan Chicken Strips

Ingredients

Vegan Chicken:

- Cooking oil spray
- 1 pound vegan chicken strips (unbreaded)
- 1 teaspoon sea salt
- ½ teaspoon dried sage
- ½ teaspoon dried thyme
- ½ teaspoon dried rosemary
- ¼ teaspoon black pepper
- 1 tablespoon olive oil

Salad:

- 4 cups spinach
- 4 cups shredded cabbage
- 1 cup thinly sliced red onions
- 1 cup shredded carrots
- 1 cup diced cucumber
- 1 cup diced celery
- 1 cup chopped pecans

Prep

1. Preheat the oven to 375 degrees. Spray a baking sheet with cooking oil or line with parchment paper. In a mixing bowl, combine the vegan chicken with the sea salt, sage, thyme, rosemary, black pepper, and olive oil. Mix all together and spread out on the baking sheet.

Cook

2. Bake for 10 minutes, or until the vegan chicken is golden brown. Allow to cool for 10 minutes.

Serve

3. Plate the spinach, shredded cabbage, and vegan chicken strips; top with red onions, carrots, cucumber, celery, and pecans.

PREP
20
MINUTES

COOK
10
MINUTES

SERVES
4

Note:

This salad pairs well with the Lemon Vinaigrette or Garlic Lime Dressing.

e2mfitness.com

Asian Chopped Salad
with Roasted Tofu

PREP
20
MINUTES

COOK
15
MINUTES

SERVES
4

Ingredients

Tofu:

- 2 (14-ounce) packages extra-firm tofu
- 1 tablespoon olive oil
- 1 teaspoon onion powder
- 1 teaspoon ground garlic
- ½ teaspoon paprika
- ½ teaspoon chili powder
- ¼ teaspoon ground cayenne pepper
- 1 teaspoon sea salt
- Cooking oil spray

Salad Base:

- 7 cups spring mix
- 1 cup thinly sliced red cabbage
- 1 cup thinly sliced green onions
- 1 cup grated carrots
- 1 cup thinly sliced celery
- 1 cup chopped peanuts
- 1 cup diced red bell peppers
- Chopped cilantro (for garnish)

Prep

1. Preheat the oven to 400 degrees. Drain and press the tofu, then cut into 1-inch cubes.

2. Prepare the seasoning mixture in a large bowl by combining the olive oil, onion powder, garlic, paprika, chili powder, cayenne, and sea salt. Add the tofu cubes and toss to coat evenly. Spray a sheet pan with cooking oil, and spread out the seasoned tofu on the pan.

Cook

3. Bake for 10 to 15 minutes, or until the tofu cubes are golden brown.

Serve

4. To assemble the salad, toss the spring mix and cabbage in a large bowl, and top with arranged rows of the prepared green onions, carrots, celery, peanuts, and red bell peppers. Add the tofu, and garnish with cilantro.

Note:

This salad pairs well with the Cilantro Lime Dressing or Garlic Lime Dressing.

Galina M., Summerville, SC

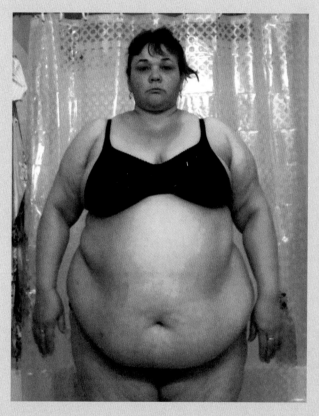
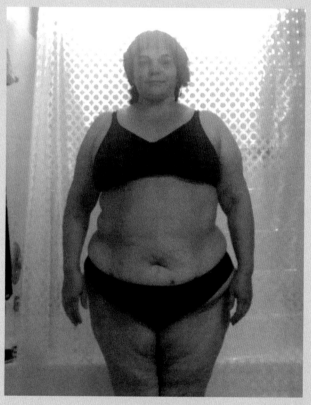

Rounds	Age	Weight Loss
5	50	70

What were you hoping to gain from your E2M fitness experience?
I was hoping to lose weight, but the more I learn, the more I realize losing weight is just one of the benefits. The program is much, much more than that. It is about adopting a new way of living.

What is your biggest E2M accomplishment?
I became coachable. I am more connected and kinder to myself than ever before.

Tofu Blueberry
Avocado Salad

Ingredients

Tofu:

- 2 (14-ounce) packages extra-firm tofu
- 1 tablespoon olive oil
- 1 teaspoon onion powder
- 1 teaspoon ground garlic
- 1 teaspoon sea salt
- ½ teaspoon paprika
- ½ teaspoon chili powder
- ¼ teaspoon ground cayenne pepper
- Cooking oil spray

Salad Base:

- 8 cups baby spinach
- 1 cup diced red onions
- 1 cup grated carrots
- 1 cup thinly sliced cucumber
- 2 avocados, peeled and diced
- 2 cups fresh blueberries
- Crushed red pepper (for garnish)

PREP
15
MINUTES

COOK
15
MINUTES

SERVES
4

Prep

1. Preheat the oven to 400 degrees. Drain the tofu, then cut into 1-inch cubes.

2. In a mixing bowl, combine the cubed tofu, olive oil, onion powder, garlic, sea salt, paprika, chili powder, and cayenne pepper; toss to coat evenly. Spray cooking oil on a sheet pan, and evenly spread out the seasoned tofu.

Cook

3. Bake the tofu for 15 minutes.

Serve

4. Put the baby spinach in a large bowl; add the red onions, carrots, cucumber, avocado, and blueberries; top with tofu and garnish with crushed red pepper.

Note:
This salad pairs well with the Lemon Vinaigrette or Cilantro Lime Dressing.

Greek Kale Salad
with Tempeh Bacon

PREP
25
MINUTES

COOK
20
MINUTES

SERVES
4

Ingredients

Tempeh:
- 1 pound tempeh
- 1 tablespoon olive oil
- 1 teaspoon onion powder
- 1 teaspoon ground garlic
- 1 teaspoon sea salt
- ½ teaspoon paprika
- ½ teaspoon mild chili powder
- ¼ teaspoon ground cayenne pepper

Salad Base:
- 8 cups baby kale
- 1 cup thinly sliced red onions
- 1 cup chopped canned artichoke hearts, drained
- 1 cup grated carrots
- 1 cup diced cucumber
- ¼ cup sliced olives

Prep

1. Preheat the oven to 400 degrees. Line a sheet pan with parchment paper. Slice the tempeh in half widthwise (so there are 2 even squares), then slice each square into 9 pieces to make a total of 18 pieces of tempeh.

2. In a shallow bowl, rimmed plate, or baking dish, whisk together the olive oil, onion powder, garlic, sea salt, paprika, chili powder, and cayenne pepper. Add the tempeh and toss to coat evenly. Arrange the tempeh in a single layer on the sheet pan.

Cook

3. Bake for 10 minutes, then flip the tempeh pieces and bake for 8 to 10 minutes more, or until browned and slightly crispy.

Serve

4. Put the baby kale in a large bowl; top with arranged rows of the prepared red onions, artichoke hearts, ½-1 cup tempeh, carrots, cucumber, and olives.

Note:
This salad pairs well with the Cilantro Lime Dressing.

Success Stories

Cheryl S., Las Vegas, NV

Rounds	Age	Weight Loss
2	56	21

COVID left me with some extra weight I wanted to lose, and a friend brought E2M fitness to my attention. We both joined. Not only did I find a workout program that worked, I also found a sense of community I'd been missing.

What does the E2M community mean to you?
I love, love, love the E2M fitness community. It's the most positive group I've ever encountered. Everyone praises even the smallest victory and uplifts everyone when there is a defeat. There's nothing like it.

Debbie O., Lyons, NY

Rounds	Age	Weight Loss
2	50	22

Non-Scale Victory (NSV)!
No swollen ankles. No protein deficiency.

What did you want to change about your lifestyle?
All-or-nothing thinking. E2M fitness teaches us to do something. And eating something doesn't mean you have to eat everything.

What is your biggest E2M fitness accomplishment?
I now control my binge eating at night.

How has the E2M fitness program changed your life?
I get up early to do the live workouts, which helps set the tone for my day.

Spicy Peanut
Edamame Salad

Ingredients

- ¼ cup Spicy Peanut Sauce (see page 129)
- Cooking oil spray
- 1 tablespoon minced garlic
- ½ teaspoon ground ginger
- 4 cups edamame
- 1 cup shredded carrots
- 4 cups cauliflower rice
- 2 limes, zested and juiced
- 1 cup diced cucumber
- 1 bunch fresh cilantro, chopped (for garnish)
- 1 tablespoon sesame seeds

Prep

1. Prepare the Spicy Peanut Sauce and set aside. Store extra in an airtight container and refrigerate for up to five days.

Cook

2. Heat a large skillet over medium heat; spray with cooking oil. Add the garlic and ginger; sauté for 2 to 3 minutes until fragrant. Add the edamame and carrots; sauté for 2 to 3 minutes until tender.

3. Add the cauliflower rice and the zest and juice of 1 lime; sauté for 3 minutes. Stir until thoroughly combined. Remove from the heat. Add the cucumber; toss to combine.

Serve

4. Plate the cauliflower rice mixture; top with fresh cilantro, sesame seeds, Spicy Peanut Sauce, and juice from the other lime.

PREP
5
MINUTES

COOK
20
MINUTES

SERVES
4

Kale Salad
with Vegan Chicken Strips

PREP
10
MINUTES

COOK
10
MINUTES

SERVES
4

Ingredients

Vegan Chicken:
- 1 pound vegan chicken strips (unbreaded)
- 1 tablespoon olive oil
- 1 teaspoon onion powder
- 1 teaspoon ground garlic
- 1 teaspoon sea salt
- ½ teaspoon paprika
- ½ teaspoon mild chili powder
- ¼ teaspoon ground cayenne pepper
- Cooking oil spray

Salad Base:
- 8 cups baby kale
- 1 cup thinly sliced red onions
- 1 cup thinly sliced bell peppers
- 1 cup grated carrots
- 2 avocados, peeled and diced
- 1 cup diced cucumber

Prep

1. In a mixing bowl, combine the vegan chicken strips with the olive oil, onion powder, garlic, sea salt, paprika, chili powder, and cayenne; mix well to coat the vegan chicken evenly.

Cook

2. Heat a skillet over medium-high heat; spray with cooking oil. Add the vegan chicken and cook for 5 to 7 minutes. Remove from the heat and allow the chicken to cool.

Serve

3. To assemble the salad, put the baby kale greens in a large bowl; top with arranged rows of thinly sliced red onions, bell peppers, vegan chicken, carrots, avocado, and cucumber.

Note:
This salad pairs well with the classic Italian Vinaigrette or Lemon Vinaigrette.

EM Success Stories

Bryant B., Killeen, TX

Rounds	Age	Weight Loss
3	50	20

After twenty-five years in the army, I retired and went through depression. At 256 pounds, I went vegan. The health benefits were my skin cleared up, no more meds for high blood pressure, no more ankle brace, and I hardly get sick! It's my lifestyle now. I know I can't beat Father Time, but I'm trying to slow him down.

What did you want to change about your lifestyle?
My four children are my why. I want to be around for them!

What does the E2M community mean to you?
Family, not judgment. You can be you.

Pamela B., Canton, NC

Rounds	Age	Weight Loss
1	41	20

Since starting the E2M fitness program, I no longer struggle with extreme fatigue and I have been able to enjoy exercising again. I have learned to eat in a way that fuels my body without counting calories or obsessing over macros.

What is your biggest E2M fitness accomplishment?
I was able to shed pounds and inflammation after a Hashimoto's hypothyroidism diagnosis. The program dialed in my eating habits and helped support things my doctors were instructing.

Non-Scale Victory (NSV)!
Lowering thyroid medication and gaining energy!

e2mfitness.com

Pecan Tofu
Citrus Salad

Ingredients

Tofu:
- 2 (14-ounce) packages extra-firm tofu
- ½ teaspoon sea salt
- ½ teaspoon black pepper
- Cooking oil spray
- 2 tablespoons Dijon mustard
- ½ cup chopped pecans
- 1 tablespoon dried thyme
- 2 tablespoons chopped fresh parsley
- 2 tablespoons orange zest (use an orange from the salad base)

Salad Base:
- 4 cups baby kale
- 4 cups shaved brussels sprouts
- 4 oranges
- 1 red onion, thinly sliced

Prep

1. Preheat the oven to 350 degrees. Line an oven-safe dish with parchment paper.

2. Drain the tofu. Stand one tofu block on the shortest side and cut down in half to yield 2 thin fillet-size pieces, about 1-inch thick; repeat with the other block of tofu. This yields 4 total fillet slices. Season the tofu slices with sea salt and black pepper.

Cook

3. Heat a pan over medium-high heat; spray with cooking oil. Sear the tofu for 1 minute; gently flip the tofu and cook for another minute. Remove the tofu and let rest to cool slightly. Spread 1½ teaspoons Dijon mustard over each piece.

4. Combine the pecans, thyme, parsley, and orange zest on a plate; roll each tofu slice in the herb-nut mixture. Put the tofu on the prepared pan; bake for 12 minutes.

5. Toss the baby kale and shaved brussels sprouts in a large bowl. Cut off the top and bottom of each orange, and peel down the sides to remove the white pith from the oranges; cut the oranges crosswise into ¼-inch-thick slices.

Serve

6. To assemble the salad, divide the kale and brussels sprouts mixture between 4 plates; add a portion of the sliced oranges and thinly sliced red onions to each serving; top with the tofu.

PREP
20
MINUTES

COOK
15
MINUTES

SERVES
4

Note:

This salad pairs well with the Spicy Balsamic Vinaigrette.

e2mfitness.com

Herb Roasted
Tofu Salad

PREP
20
MINUTES

COOK
15
MINUTES

SERVES
4

Ingredients

Tofu:

- 2 (14-ounce) packages extra-firm tofu
- 1 teaspoon dried rosemary
- 1 teaspoon dried thyme
- 1 teaspoon chopped fresh chives

- 1 teaspoon sea salt
- ¼ teaspoon black pepper
- 2 tablespoons Dijon mustard
- Cooking oil spray
- 1½ cups sliced button mushrooms

Salad Base:

- 4 cups baby kale
- 4 cups broccoli slaw

- 1 cup sliced English cucumber
- 1 cup thinly sliced red onions

Prep

1. Preheat the oven to 350 degrees. Spray a baking dish with cooking oil.

2. Drain the tofu. Stand one tofu block on the shortest side and cut down in half to yield 2 thin fillet-size pieces, about 1-inch thick; repeat with the other block of tofu. This yields 4 total fillet slices.

3. Combine the rosemary, thyme, chives, sea salt, and black pepper. Brush the top and sides of each tofu slice with 1½ teaspoons of Dijon mustard, then season with the herb mixture.

Cook

4. Heat a skillet over medium-high heat; spray with cooking oil. Sear the tofu slices for 1 minute; gently flip the fillets and cook for another minute. Remove the tofu from the pan; sauté the mushrooms for 2 minutes.

5. Transfer the mushrooms to the prepared baking dish, and put the tofu on top of the mushrooms. Bake for 10 minutes.

Serve

6. Toss the kale and broccoli slaw in a large bowl. Top with cucumber, red onions, mushrooms, and tofu.

Note:

This salad pairs well with the Spicy Balsamic Vinaigrette or Red Pepper Dressing.

Buffalo Vegan Chicken
Salad

Ingredients

Salad Base:
- 7 cups shredded cabbage
- 1 cup diced celery
- 1½ cups shredded carrots
- 2 avocados, peeled and diced
- 2 tablespoons Buffalo Seasoning (see page 125)
- ¼ cup chopped cilantro
- "Ranch" Seasoning (see page 119)

Vegan Chicken:
- 1 pound vegan chicken strips (unbreaded)
- 1 tablespoon olive oil

Prep

1. For the salad base, combine the cabbage, celery, and carrots in a large bowl.

2. Prepare the "Ranch" Seasoning in a small bowl by combining the garlic, thyme, parsley, dill, cilantro, sea salt, and black pepper; mix well. Add 2 tablespoons of the blend to the salad base, and toss to mix. Store the extra seasoning blend in an airtight container.

3. For the Buffalo Seasoning, combine the chili powder, paprika, onion powder, garlic, sea salt, black pepper, and optional cayenne pepper; mix well. Add the vegan chicken strips to the bowl, and toss to combine.

Cook

4. Heat the olive oil in a large nonstick skillet over medium heat. Add the seasoned vegan chicken strips; cook for 5 to 7 minutes, stirring frequently. Once cooked, set aside to cool.

Serve

5. Plate the cabbage mixture; top with the vegan chicken and diced avocado. Garnish with fresh cilantro.

PREP
20
MINUTES

COOK
10
MINUTES

SERVES
4

Note:

This salad pairs well with the Vegan "Ranch" Dressing.

e2mfitness.com

Mandarin Vegan
Chicken Salad

PREP
20
MINUTES

COOK
10
MINUTES

SERVES
4

Ingredients

Vegan Chicken:

- 1 pound vegan chicken strips (unbreaded)
- 1 tablespoon lemon pepper
- 1 tablespoon olive oil
- 1 teaspoon dried basil
- 1 teaspoon dried oregano
- 1 teaspoon sea salt
- ½ teaspoon dried thyme
- Cooking oil spray

Salad Base:

- 8 cups spinach
- ¼ cup thinly sliced green onions
- 1 cup diced cucumber
- 4 mandarins, peeled and separated
- ½ cup slivered almonds
- Black and white sesame seeds (for garnish)
- ½ teaspoon red pepper flakes (optional)

Prep

1. Preheat the oven to 400 degrees. Combine the vegan chicken strips, lemon pepper, olive oil, basil, oregano, sea salt, and thyme; mix well to coat the vegan chicken evenly. Spray a sheet pan with cooking oil, and put the seasoned vegan chicken strips on the pan.

Cook

2. Bake for 10 minutes. Allow the vegan chicken to rest for 10 minutes to cool, then dice to prepare for the salad.

Serve

3. To assemble the salad, put the spinach in a large bowl; add the green onions, cucumber, mandarin orange segments, and slivered almonds; top with vegan chicken and then sesame seeds for garnish.

Note:

This salad pairs well with the Red Pepper Dressing or Cilantro Lime Dressing.

Warm Mediterranean
Edamame Salad

PREP
5
MINUTES

COOK
20
MINUTES

SERVES
4

Ingredients

- 2 tablespoons Mediterranean Seasoning (see page 118)
- Cooking oil spray
- ½ cup diced red onions
- 1 red bell pepper, thinly sliced
- 4 cups edamame

- 4 cups shredded cabbage
- 1 lemon, zested and juiced
- 1 cup slivered almonds
- 1 tablespoon chopped fresh basil
- ½ teaspoon sea salt
- ¼ teaspoon black pepper

Prep

1. Combine ingredients for the Mediterranean Seasoning and set aside. Store extra in an airtight container.

Cook

2. Heat a large skillet over medium heat; spray with cooking oil. Add the red onions and bell peppers; sauté for 5 to 8 minutes, or until tender. Add the edamame and Mediterranean Seasoning; sauté for 2 to 3 minutes, or until the edamame is tender and bright green.

3. In a large bowl, combine the shredded cabbage with the lemon zest and juice; toss to mix thoroughly.

Serve

4. Plate the cabbage; top with sautéed red onions, peppers, and edamame. Garnish with slivered almonds and fresh basil.

Note:
This salad is also delicious served cold and even better the next day!

"Ranch" Tempeh
Salad

Ingredients

Tempeh:

- 1 pound tempeh, cut into 1-inch cubes
- 1 tablespoon olive oil
- 1 cucumber, sliced
- ½ red onion, finely diced

- 1 tablespoon rice vinegar
- 1 tablespoon Everything but the Bagel seasoning
- Cooking oil spray
- "Ranch" Seasoning (see page 119)

Salad Base:

- 8 cups spring mix
- 2 avocados, peeled and diced

- 1 cup mandarin orange segments
- 1 lime, zested and juiced

Prep

1. Prepare the "Ranch" Seasoning in a large bowl by combining the garlic, parsley, dill, thyme, lime zest, lime juice, sea salt, and black pepper. Add the tempeh and olive oil; toss to coat evenly.

2. In a separate bowl, combine the prepared cucumber and red onions with the rice vinegar and Everything but the Bagel seasoning; refrigerate until ready to serve.

Cook

3. Heat a pan over medium heat; spray with cooking oil. Sauté the cubed tempeh for 5 to 7 minutes.

Serve

4. Plate the cucumber and onion mixture with the seasoned tempeh, spring mix, and diced avocado. Top with mandarin orange slices, lime zest, and lime juice.

PREP **20** MINUTES

COOK **10** MINUTES

SERVES **4**

Note:

This salad pairs well with the Vegan "Ranch" Dressing.

e2mfitness.com

Cilantro Lime
Tempeh Salad

PREP
15
MINUTES

COOK
10
MINUTES

SERVES
4

Ingredients

Tempeh:
- Cooking oil spray
- 1 pound tempeh, cut into 1-inch cubes
- 1 tablespoon olive oil
- ½ teaspoon sea salt
- ⅛ teaspoon black pepper

Salad Base:
- 6 cups chopped spinach
- 2 cups arugula
- 1 cup diced red bell peppers
- 1 cup diced red onions
- 1 cucumber, diced
- 2 avocados, peeled and diced
- 1 lime, juiced
- 2 tablespoons chopped cilantro

Prep

1. Preheat the oven to 400 degrees. Spray cooking oil on a sheet pan or line with parchment paper. In a bowl, combine the tempeh, olive oil, sea salt, and black pepper; toss to coat evenly, then spread out the cubes on the prepared pan.

Cook

2. Bake for 10 minutes. Allow the tempeh to cool before adding to the salad.

Serve

3. Toss the spinach, arugula, red peppers, red onions, cucumber, avocado, and tempeh; divide between the plates. Top with a squeeze of lime juice and some fresh cilantro.

Note:
This salad pairs well with Cilantro Lime Dressing or Red Pepper Dressing.

Peach Tofu
Salad

PREP
25
MINUTES

COOK
10
MINUTES

SERVES
4

Note:

The cucumber, celery, and basil salad of this main dish is a healthy side dish that's easy to make!

This salad pairs well with the Lemon Vinaigrette or Avocado Lime Dressing.

Ingredients

Tofu:
- 2 (14-ounce) packages extra-firm tofu
- 1 lemon, zested and juiced
- 1 tablespoon olive oil
- ½ teaspoon ground garlic
- ¼ teaspoon crushed red pepper
- ½ teaspoon sea salt
- ⅛ teaspoon black pepper
- Cooking oil spray

Salad Base:
- 2 cucumbers, halved, seeded (if preferred), and sliced
- 2 cups diced celery
- ¼ cup chopped fresh basil
- ¼ teaspoon sesame seeds (optional)
- ⅛ teaspoon crushed red pepper (optional)
- Cooking oil spray
- 2 peaches, pitted and sliced
- 2 avocados, peeled and diced

Prep

1. Drain and press the tofu, then cut into 1-inch cubes. In a large bowl, whisk together the lemon zest, lemon juice, olive oil, garlic, crushed red pepper, sea salt, and black pepper. Add the cubed tofu and toss to coat evenly; refrigerate for 30 minutes.

2. Combine the cucumber, celery, and basil with the optional sesame seeds and crushed red pepper, if desired; toss to mix well.

Cook

3. Heat a pan over medium heat; spray with cooking oil. Sauté the peaches for 2 to 3 minutes and remove from the pan.

4. Spray the pan again with cooking oil; sauté the cubed tofu for 5 to 7 minutes.

Serve

5. Plate the cucumber salad, and top with a portion of the tofu, sautéed peaches, and diced avocado.

Sonoma Vegan
Chicken Salad

Ingredients

Chicken:

- 1 pound vegan chicken strips (unbreaded)
- 1 tablespoon olive oil
- 1 tablespoon dried basil
- 1 tablespoon dried rosemary
- Cooking oil spray
- ½ teaspoon sea salt
- ½ teaspoon black pepper

Salad Base:

- 2 cups finely chopped romaine
- 2 cups shredded cabbage or slaw mixture
- 1 cup chopped apples
- ½ cup finely chopped celery
- ½ cup chopped red onions
- ½ lemon, juiced
- ½ cup chopped pecans

Prep

1. In a bowl, combine the vegan chicken, olive oil, basil, and rosemary; toss to coat evenly.

Cook

2. Heat a skillet over medium-high heat; spray with cooking oil. Sauté the vegan chicken strips for 5 to 7 minutes. Once cooled, shred the strips or chop into bite-size pieces.

Serve

3. Combine the romaine and cabbage in a large bowl, then add the vegan chicken and prepared apples, celery, red onions, and lemon juice. Toss to combine, and top with pecans.

PREP
20
MINUTES

COOK
10
MINUTES

SERVES
4

Note:

This salad pairs well with the Chipotle Chimichurri Vinaigrette or Red Pepper Dressing.

e2mfitness.com

Mediterranean Tofu
Salad

PREP
30
MINUTES

COOK
10
MINUTES

SERVES
4

Ingredients

Tofu:
- 2 (14-ounce) packages extra-firm tofu
- 1 lemon, zested and juiced
- 2 tablespoons olive oil
- ½ teaspoon ground garlic
- ½ teaspoon dried rosemary
- ½ teaspoon dried oregano
- ¼ teaspoon crushed red pepper
- ¼ teaspoon sea salt
- ⅛ teaspoon black pepper
- Cooking oil spray

Salad base:
- 4 cups baby kale
- 4 cups packaged broccoli slaw
- 1⅓ cups chopped red bell peppers
- 1⅓ cups chopped mushrooms
- 1⅓ cups chopped canned artichokes hearts, drained

Prep

1. Drain and press the tofu, then cut into 1-inch cubes. In a large bowl, whisk together the lemon zest, lemon juice, olive oil, garlic, rosemary, oregano, crushed red pepper, sea salt, and black pepper. Add the cubed tofu and toss to coat evenly; refrigerate for 30 minutes.

Cook

2. Heat a pan over medium heat; spray with cooking oil. Sauté the cubed tofu for 5 to 7 minutes, then remove from the heat and set aside.

Serve

3. Plate the kale and broccoli slaw. Top each serving with tofu and a portion of the prepared red bell peppers, mushrooms, and artichokes.

Note:
This salad pairs well with the Italian Vinaigrette.

Smoothies & Oats

Happy Viking
Created by Tennis Champ Venus Williams

"When I was diagnosed with a career-ending autoimmune disease, I could barely walk, much less play tennis. After plant-based superfoods transformed my health, I made them part of my daily routine and went on to win a total of 75 championships over a 25-year career. Those recipes become the blueprint for Happy Viking: the all-in-one meal that will change your life in two delicious scoops."

—Venus Williams

Mango
Coconut Smoothie

Ingredients

- 12 ounces unsweetened coconut milk
- 1 serving piña colada protein powder
- 1 teaspoon grated fresh ginger
- ¼ teaspoon ground turmeric
- ¼ teaspoon ground cardamom
- 1 cup frozen mango

Prep & Serve

Combine all ingredients in a blender and blend until smooth. Pour and enjoy!

Chocolate Peanut
Butter Cup Smoothie

Ingredients

- 12 ounces unsweetened dairy-free milk
- 1 serving chocolate protein powder
- ½ teaspoon ground cinnamon
- 1 tablespoon peanut butter

Prep & Serve

Combine all ingredients in a blender and blend until smooth. Pour and enjoy!

Chocolate Covered
Raspberry Smoothie

Ingredients

- 12 ounces unsweetened dairy-free milk
- 1 serving chocolate protein powder
- ½ teaspoon ground cinnamon
- ½ avocado, peeled
- 1 cup frozen raspberries
- Ice

Prep & Serve

Combine all ingredients in a blender and blend until smooth. Pour and enjoy!

PREP
5
MINUTES

SERVES
1

Strawberry Shortcake
Smoothie Bowl

Ingredients

- ¾ cup unsweetened dairy-free milk or water
- 1 serving vanilla protein powder
- 1 cup frozen strawberries
- 1 tablespoon almond butter
- ½ teaspoon ground cinnamon
- Fresh strawberries (for garnish)
- ¼ cup peanuts, finely chopped

Prep & Serve

Combine the dairy-free milk, protein powder, frozen strawberries, almond butter, and cinnamon in a blender; blend until smooth. Pour into a bowl and top with fresh strawberries and chopped peanuts.

PREP
5
MINUTES

SERVES
1

e2mfitness.com

Peaches and Cream
Smoothie Bowl

PREP
5
MINUTES

SERVES
1

Ingredients

- 6 ounces unsweetened dairy-free milk
- 1 serving vanilla protein powder
- 1 cup sliced frozen peaches
- 1 peeled and sliced frozen banana
- Fresh peach slices (for garnish)
- 1 tablespoon Homemade Granola (see page 105)

Prep & Serve

Combine the dairy-free milk, protein powder, frozen peaches, and frozen banana chunks in a blender; blend until smooth.
Pour into a bowl and top with fresh peach slices and Homemade Granola.

Chocolate Pecan Pie
Smoothie Bowl

PREP
5
MINUTES

SERVES
1

Ingredients

- 6 ounces unsweetened dairy-free milk or water
- 1 serving chocolate protein powder
- 1 tablespoon nut butter
- ½ teaspoon ground cinnamon
- ¼ cup pecans, finely chopped
- 2 tablespoons Homemade Granola (see page 105)

Prep & Serve

Combine the dairy-free milk, protein powder, nut butter, and cinnamon in a blender; blend until smooth.
Pour into a bowl and top with chopped pecans and Homemade Granola.

Strawberry Banana
Smoothie

PREP
5
MINUTES

SERVES
1

Ingredients

- 12 ounces unsweetened dairy-free milk or water
- ½ cup frozen strawberries
- 1 serving strawberry protein powder
- 1 peeled and sliced frozen banana

Prep & Serve

Combine all ingredients in a blender and blend until smooth.
Pour and enjoy!

Vanilla Salted
Caramel Smoothie

Ingredients

- 12 ounces unsweetened coconut milk
- 1 serving vanilla protein powder
- ⅛ teaspoon sea salt
- 1 tablespoon peanut butter or peanut butter powder
- Ice

Prep & Serve

Combine all ingredients in a blender and blend until smooth. Pour and enjoy!

PREP
5
MINUTES

SERVES
1

Mocha Latte
Smoothie

Ingredients

- 8 ounces unsweetened coconut milk or dairy free milk
- 4 ounces cold-brew coffee
- 1 serving chocolate protein powder
- 1 teaspoon ground cinnamon
- Ice

Prep & Serve

Combine all ingredients in a blender and blend until smooth. Pour and enjoy!

PREP
5
MINUTES

SERVES
1

e2mfitness.com

Overnight Oats

Overnight oats are an excellent choice for breakfast meal prep. Mix up one of these recipes the night before and have breakfast on the go! You can use a variety of fruits and spice combinations to change up the flavor profile.

E2M Fitness supports our female members during their postpartum journey. These overnight and baked oats recipes provide a strong foundation for our moms as they begin to work on their personal health and wellness after delivering their new treasures!

Pumpkin Pie
Baked Oats

Ingredients

- Cooking oil spray
- 1 cup old-fashioned oats
- 1 serving vanilla protein powder
- ½ teaspoon baking powder
- 1 teaspoon ground cinnamon
- ¼ teaspoon ground nutmeg

- 1 banana, peeled
- 2 tablespoons pumpkin puree
- ¾ cup unsweetened coconut milk or other dairy-free milk
- Homemade Granola (see page 105)

Prep

1. Preheat the oven to 325 degrees unless using the microwave. Spray a single-serve baking dish or coffee mug with cooking oil.

2. Combine the oats, protein powder, baking powder, cinnamon, and nutmeg in a blender; pulse to make a powder. Add the banana, pumpkin, and coconut milk; blend until smooth.

Cook

3. Pour the batter in the prepared dish; bake for 20 minutes or microwave on high for 4 minutes. Top with Homemade Granola.

Serve

4. Allow to cool and dig in!

PREP
5
MINUTES

COOK
20
MINUTES

SERVES
1

Banana Nut
Baked Oats

PREP
5
MINUTES

COOK
20
MINUTES

SERVES
1

Ingredients

- Cooking oil spray
- 1 cup old-fashioned oats
- 1 serving vanilla protein powder
- ½ teaspoon baking powder

- 1 banana, peeled (reserve a few slices for topping)
- 1 tablespoon nut butter
- ¾ cup unsweetened coconut milk or other dairy-free milk

Prep

1. Preheat the oven to 325 degrees unless using the microwave. Spray a single-serve baking dish or coffee mug with cooking oil.

2. Combine the oats, protein powder, and baking powder in a blender; pulse to make a powder. Add the banana (reserve a few slices), nut butter, and coconut milk; blend until smooth.

Cook

3. Pour the batter in the prepared dish; bake for 20 minutes or microwave on high for 4 minutes. Top with the reserved banana slices.

Serve

4. Allow to cool and dig in!

Chocolate Peanut
Butter Overnight Oats

Ingredients

Oats:

- 12 ounces unsweetened dairy-free milk
- 1 serving chocolate protein powder
- ½ teaspoon vanilla extract
- 1 teaspoon peanut butter
- 1 cup old-fashioned oats, divided
- 1 tablespoon chia seeds, divided
- 1 tablespoon peanut butter

Topping:

- 1 tablespoon chopped roasted peanuts, divided

Prep

1. Whisk together the dairy-free milk, protein powder, and vanilla in a bowl until the mixture is well combined and the protein powder is dissolved. Add the peanut butter and stir until smooth; set aside to add to the oats later.

2. Arrange two small, sealable containers (such as canning jars or plastic containers), then add ½ cup oats and 1½ teaspoons chia seeds to each container. Divide the liquid mixture into two servings; pour over the oats and stir to combine.

3. Top each serving 1½ teaspoons chopped peanuts. Seal each container and refrigerate overnight or at least 4 hours.

Serve

4. Remove the overnight oats from the refrigerator and enjoy!

Vanilla Lemon Berry
Overnight Oats

PREP
5
MINUTES

SERVES
2

Ingredients

- 12 ounces unsweetened dairy-free milk
- 1 serving vanilla protein powder
- ½ teaspoon vanilla extract
- ½ teaspoon lemon zest, divided
- 1 cup old-fashioned oats, divided
- 1 tablespoon chia seeds, divided
- 1 cup blueberries, divided

Prep

1. Whisk together the dairy-free milk, protein powder, vanilla, and ¼ teaspoon lemon zest in a bowl until the mixture is well combined and the protein powder is dissolved; set aside to add to the oats later.

2. Arrange two small, sealable containers (such as canning jars or plastic containers), then add ½ cup oats and 1½ teaspoons chia seeds to each container. Divide the liquid mixture into two servings; pour over the oats and stir to combine.

3. Top each serving with ¼ cup blueberries. Seal each container and refrigerate overnight or at least 4 hours.

Serve

4. Remove the overnight oats from the refrigerator; top each serving with ⅛ teaspoon lemon zest.

Strawberry Crunch
Overnight Oats

PREP
5
MINUTES

SERVES
2

Ingredients

- 12 ounces unsweetened dairy-free milk
- 1 serving strawberry protein powder
- ½ teaspoon vanilla extract

- 1 cup old-fashioned oats, divided
- 1 tablespoon chia seeds, divided
- 1 cup diced strawberries, divided
- 2 tablespoons Homemade Granola (see page 105), divided

Prep

1. Whisk together the dairy-free milk, protein powder, and vanilla in a bowl until the mixture is well combined and the protein powder is dissolved; set aside to add to the oats later.

2. Arrange two small, sealable containers (such as canning jars or plastic containers), then add ½ cup oats and 1½ teaspoons chia seeds to each container. Divide the liquid mixture into two servings; pour over the oats and stir to combine.

3. Top each serving with ½ cup diced strawberries. Seal each container and refrigerate overnight or at least 4 hours.

Serve

4. Remove the overnight oats from the refrigerator; top each serving with 1 tablespoon Homemade Granola.

Piña Colada
Overnight Oats

PREP
5
MINUTES

SERVES
2

Ingredients

- 12 ounces unsweetened dairy-free milk
- 1 serving piña colada protein powder
- ½ teaspoon vanilla extract
- 1 cup old-fashioned oats, divided
- 1 tablespoon chia seeds, divided
- 1 cup diced pineapple, divided
- 2 tablespoons toasted coconut flakes, divided

Prep

1. Whisk together the dairy-free milk, protein powder, and vanilla in a bowl until the mixture is well combined and the protein powder is dissolved; set aside to add to the oats later.

2. Arrange two small, sealable containers (such as canning jars or plastic containers), then add ½ cup oats, 1½ teaspoons chia seeds, and ¼ cup pineapple to each container. Divide the liquid mixture into two servings; pour over the oats and stir to combine.

3. Top each serving with another ¼ cup pineapple. Seal each container and refrigerate overnight or at least 4 hours.

Serve

4. Remove the overnight oats from the refrigerator; top each serving with 1 tablespoon toasted coconut.

Homemade
Granola

Ingredients

- 1½ cups old-fashioned oats
- ½ cup sliced almonds
- ½ cup pecans, chopped
- ⅓ cup shredded unsweetened coconut
- ½ cup nut or seed butter
- ½ teaspoon vanilla extract
- 1 teaspoon ground cinnamon
- ¼ teaspoon ground nutmeg
- ½ cup golden raisins

Prep

1. Move an oven rack to the lowest position, then preheat the oven to 325 degrees. Line a baking sheet with parchment paper.

2. Combine the oats, almonds, pecans, and coconut in a large mixing bowl. In a separate bowl, combine the nut butter, vanilla, cinnamon, and nutmeg; stir until evenly incorporated.

3. Fold the nut butter mixture into the oats mixture; stir until well combined. Transfer the granola to the prepared baking sheet and spread in an even layer.

Cook

4. Bake the granola for 20 minutes. Remove the pan and use a spatula to toss the granola. Return the pan to the oven; bake for an additional 6 to 7 minutes, until the coconut is golden brown.

5. Allow the granola to cool, then stir in the raisins. Use as a tasty topping for the smoothie bowls or overnight oats recipes.

Storage

6. Store the granola in an airtight container for up to seven days.

PREP
10
MINUTES

COOK
30
MINUTES

YIELD
3½
CUPS

Dressings made from scratch are versatile and simple to make at home. Any of these dressing recipes can also be used as marinades for your proteins. These ingredients are used in many other recipes, so go ahead and buy in bulk to stock your pantry!

Another major benefit of homemade dressings is that they are free of preservatives, added sugars, and artificial flavorings. The more you know, the more you grow!

Dressings

Italian Vinaigrette

½ cup extra-virgin olive oil
2 tablespoons red wine vinegar
1 teaspoon Dijon mustard
¼ teaspoon dried parsley
¼ teaspoon dried oregano
2 fresh garlic cloves, minced
⅛ teaspoon crushed red pepper
¼ teaspoon sea salt
⅛ teaspoon black pepper

Combine all ingredients in a mason jar, secure the lid, and shake. Store in an airtight container in the refrigerator for up to three days.

Chipotle Chimichurri Vinaigrette

½ cup extra virgin olive oil
2 tablespoons fresh lime juice
2 tablespoons red wine vinegar
2 fresh garlic cloves, minced
¼ cup fresh flat-leaf parsley, chopped
½ cup fresh cilantro, chopped
¼ teaspoon sea salt
¼ teaspoon ground chipotle seasoning

Combine all ingredients in a blender. Blend until smooth. Store in an airtight container in the refrigerator for up to three days.

Chef Note: pairs deliciously with chicken or beef.

Lemon Vinaigrette

½ cup extra-virgin olive oil
3 tablespoons fresh lemon juice
1 teaspoon Dijon mustard
2 fresh garlic cloves, minced
¼ teaspoon sea salt
⅛ teaspoon black pepper

Combine all ingredients in a mason jar, secure the lid, and shake. Store in an airtight container in the refrigerator for up to three days.

Red Pepper Dressing

½ cup extra-virgin olive oil
½ cup canned roasted red peppers, drained
¼ cup lemon juice
1 tablespoon Dijon mustard
1 fresh garlic clove, minced
½ teaspoon sea salt
¼ teaspoon black pepper

Combine all ingredients in a blender. Blend until smooth. Store in an airtight container in the refrigerator for up to three days.

Aimee B., San Antonio, TX

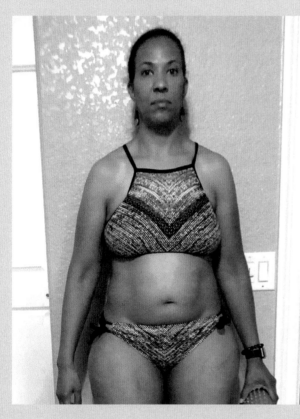 

Rounds	Age	Weight Loss
6	45	20

I am a physician and a single mom with three young kids. I lacked the practical plan and community to create the healthy life I wanted. The E2M fitness program gave me both, and I have not looked back almost two years later.

Non-Scale Victory (NSV)!
I have created a lifestyle that includes a nutritious diet and daily exercise. I have become an example of health for my boys and my patients.

What is your favorite type of workout?
The HIIT circuits are short and effective and have become my non-negotiable for the week.

Cilantro Lime Dressing

½ cup extra-virgin olive oil
2 tablespoons fresh lime juice
1 tablespoon apple cider vinegar
1 teaspoon fresh garlic, minced
¼ cup fresh cilantro, chopped
¼ teaspoon sea salt
⅛ teaspoon black pepper

Combine all ingredients in a blender. Blend until smooth. Store in an airtight container in the refrigerator for up to three days.

Garlic Lime Dressing

½ cup extra-virgin olive oil
1 tablespoon rice vinegar
1 teaspoon ground garlic
1 teaspoon fresh parsley
1 teaspoon dried dill
2 limes, zest and juice
¼ teaspoon sea salt
⅛ teaspoon black pepper

Combine all ingredients in a mason jar (only the zest and juice from the lime are used), secure the lid, and shake. Store in an airtight container in the refrigerator for up to three days.

E2M Success Stories

Tracey C., Hanahan, SC

Rounds	Age	Weight Loss
9	49	12

I am a full-time public educator who is passionate about teaching and empowering my students and their families. Through the E2M fitness program, I now have the most energy, self-confidence, and endurance to live my fullest life! I've gained the most incredible friendships.

What is your favorite type of workout?
Spin and Spartan races.

How has the E2M fitness program changed your life?
I have a genuine connection with the kindest and most energetic people who believe in me and our passion for healthy and vibrant living!

Kara G., Panama, NY

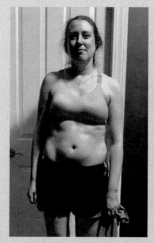 

Rounds	Age	Weight Loss
8	44	25

The positivity and discipline I've gained in the E2M fitness program has carried over to other aspects of my life, both personally and professionally! I was hoping to get "in shape." I got that and so much more! I'm never going back.

What is your favorite type of workout?
I love the E2M spin classes. Love to the spin crew and coaches!

What did you want to change about your lifestyle?
I wanted to feel good about eating vegan food and get back into a regular workout routine.

Non-Scale Victory (NSV)!
Gaining back my confidence.

Spicy Balsamic Vinaigrette

3 tablespoons balsamic vinegar
½ cup extra-virgin olive oil
1 tablespoon Dijon mustard
1 teaspoon ground garlic
⅛ teaspoon chipotle seasoning
¼ teaspoon sea salt
⅛ teaspoon black pepper

Combine all ingredients in a mason jar, secure the lid, and shake. Store in an airtight container in the refrigerator for up to three days.

Avocado Lime Dressing

½ cup extra-virgin olive oil
1 avocado, peeled and diced
3 tablespoons lime juice
1 tablespoon apple cider vinegar
¼ cup cilantro, chopped
1 teaspoon Dijon mustard
¼ teaspoon sea salt
⅛ teaspoon black pepper

Combine all ingredients in a blender. Blend until smooth. Store in an airtight container in the refrigerator for up to three days.

Creamy Tahini Dressing

¼ cup water
¼ cup tahini
3 tablespoons lemon juice
1 fresh garlic clove, minced
½ teaspoon Dijon mustard
¼ teaspoon sea salt
⅛ teaspoon black pepper

Combine all ingredients in a blender.
Blend until smooth. Store in an airtight
container in the refrigerator for up to
three days.

Vegan "Ranch" Dressing

½ cup extra-virgin olive oil
¼ cup rice wine vinegar
1 teaspoon ground garlic
1 tablespoon fresh parsley
1 teaspoon dried dill
¼ teaspoon dried thyme
1 lime, zest and juice
1 tablespoon chopped fresh cilantro
¼ teaspoon sea salt
⅛ teaspoon black pepper

Combine all ingredients in a blender (only the
zest and juice from the lime are used). Blend
until smooth. Store in an airtight container in the
refrigerator for up to three days.

Thai Peanut Dressing

¼ cup peanut butter
3 tablespoons lime juice
1 tablespoon coconut aminos
2 teaspoons fresh grated ginger
½ teaspoon chili paste
1 garlic clove, minced
¼ teaspoon sea salt
⅛ teaspoon black pepper

Combine all ingredients in a blender. Blend until smooth. Add water as needed to thin the sauce to your desired consistency. Season with sea salt and black pepper. Store in an airtight container in the refrigerator for up to three days.

Join us in making your own spice blends at home using these great recipes. Homemade spice blends do not contain any preservatives and can be used in a variety of ways. For each unique blend, mix together all the ingredients in a small bowl. Transfer to an airtight container or jar. You can store these seasoning mixes up to one year in a cool, dry place. Try Chef Jennie's favorite way to utilize spice blends: combine a seasoning blend with oil and vinegar to create your own salad dressing!

Spice Blends

Spices

Mediterranean Blend

1 tablespoon ground garlic
1½ teaspoon sea salt
1½ teaspoons dried rosemary
1½ teaspoons dried oregano
1½ teaspoons black pepper
1½ teaspoons lemon zest

Ginger Garlic Blend

3 tablespoons ground ginger
1½ tablespoons ground garlic
1 tablespoon black pepper
1 teaspoon sea salt

Lemon Pepper Seasoning

3 tablespoons lemon zest
1½ tablespoons ground
    rainbow peppercorn
1½ teaspoons onion powder
1½ teaspoons ground garlic

Chili-Lime Seasoning

1½ teaspoons smoked paprika
1½ teaspoons ground garlic
1½ teaspoons black pepper
1½ teaspoons dried oregano
¾ teaspoon ground
    cayenne pepper
1 tablespoon sea salt
1 tablespoon chili powder
Zest from 1 lime

Herbs de Provence Seasoning

2 tablespoons dried thyme
2 tablespoons dried basil
1 tablespoon dried oregano
2 teaspoons dried rosemary
1 teaspoon dried tarragon

"Ranch" Seasoning

1½ tablespoons ground garlic
1 tablespoon dried thyme
1 tablespoon dried parsley
1 tablespoon dried dill
1 tablespoon dried cilantro
⅛ teaspoon sea salt
⅛ teaspoon black pepper

Jerk Seasoning

1 tablespoon ground garlic
2 teaspoons ground cayenne pepper
2 teaspoons onion powder
2 teaspoons dried thyme
2 teaspoons dried parsley
2 teaspoons sea salt
1 teaspoon paprika
1 teaspoon ground allspice
½ teaspoon black pepper
½ teaspoon crushed red pepper
½ teaspoon ground nutmeg
¼ teaspoon ground cinnamon

Peri Peri Blend

2 teaspoons paprika
2 teaspoons ground cayenne pepper
2 teaspoons ground garlic
2 teaspoons dried oregano
1 teaspoon sea salt
1 teaspoon crushed red pepper
½ teaspoon ground cinnamon
½ teaspoon ground cardamom
½ teaspoon ground ginger

≣M Success Stories

Rhett A., Charleston, SC

Rounds	Age	Weight Loss
2	47	15

A few years ago, I was diagnosed with a rare, life-threatening disease that turned my family's lives upside down. This led me to eating a vegan diet, but I wasn't eating very clean or healthy. I tried several programs, but nothing worked until the E2M fitness program, and now I'm creating my own health story. In round two, I focused on my mental and spiritual needs, which led me to a more disciplined lifestyle. I honestly didn't realize I had an unhealthy relationship with food until this program.

What is your favorite type of workout?
Circuits and Whit's glute program.

LaTasha H., Richmond, VA

Rounds	Age	Weight Loss
4	41	30

What is your biggest E2M fitness accomplishment?
I went from a completely sedentary lifestyle to working out six days a week.

What were you hoping to gain from your E2M experience?
I was hoping to lose a lot of weight and to maintain a healthy weight and lifestyle.

How has the E2M fitness program changed your life?
It has given me confidence and the tools to maintain a healthy lifestyle. I have also developed a love for exercising.

e2mfitness.com

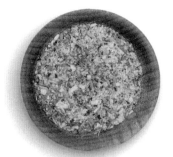

Lemon Basil Seasoning

2 tablespoons lemon zest
1 tablespoon dried basil
2 teaspoons sea salt
2 teaspoons ground garlic
1 teaspoon dried thyme
1 teaspoon black pepper

Cajun Blend

2½ teaspoons paprika
2 teaspoons ground garlic
1½ teaspoons sea salt
1¼ teaspoons dried oregano
1¼ teaspoons dried thyme
1 teaspoon onion powder
1 teaspoon ground
    cayenne pepper
1 teaspoon black pepper
½ teaspoon crushed red pepper

Spicy BBQ Rub

1 tablespoon chili powder
1 tablespoon ground garlic
¾ teaspoon ground cumin
¾ teaspoon ground mustard
¾ teaspoon sea salt
½ teaspoon black pepper
½ teaspoon cayenne pepper
½ teaspoon crushed red pepper
½ teaspoon chipotle seasoning

Smoked Chili Seasoning

2 tablespoons chili powder
1 tablespoon smoked paprika
1 tablespoon ground cumin
1 tablespoon dried oregano
1 tablespoon ground garlic
1 tablespoon onion powder

Vanecia C., Fort Mill, SC

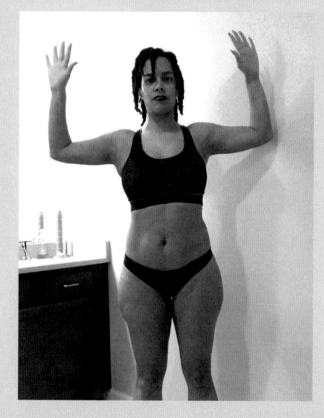 

Rounds	Age	Weight Loss
10	38	30

What is your biggest accomplishment through the E2M program?
Finding a strength in me after a back injury that I thought I would never get back. I've got the body I've always dreamed of and the confidence to match.

How has E2M fitness changed your life?
E2M fitness is now my way of life. I don't even think about it as a diet or a program. It's just how I live. And for that, I'm forever grateful.

Non-Scale Victory (NSV)!
I sleep better and no longer have migraines!

Everything Seasoning

2 tablespoons ground garlic
2 tablespoons onion powder
½ teaspoon poppy seeds
½ teaspoon sesame seeds
½ teaspoon black pepper
¼ teaspoon sea salt

Southwestern Seasoning

2 tablespoons chili powder
1 tablespoon ground cumin
1 tablespoon dried oregano
1 tablespoon ground garlic
1 tablespoon onion powder

Asian Spice Blend

1½ tablespoons ground garlic
1½ teaspoons sea salt
1½ teaspoons ground ginger
1½ teaspoons crushed red pepper
1½ teaspoons black pepper
1½ teaspoons onion powder

Lemon Herb Spice Blend

2 teaspoons paprika
2 teaspoons dried rosemary
1 teaspoon sea salt
1 teaspoon black pepper
½ teaspoon ground garlic
½ teaspoon dried parsley
½ teaspoon ground mustard
½ teaspoon onion powder
Zest from 1 lemon

Deidre C., Johns Creek, GA

Rounds	Age	Weight Loss
3	54	40.1

Non-Scale Victory (NSV)!
Rebuilding and regaining physical strength. I have gained so much more confidence.

What did you want to change about your lifestyle?
I just wanted to feel better overall. I knew that weight loss would be a big step to feeling better, looking better, and even sleeping better.

What is your favorite type of workout?
The E2M fitness high intensity type workouts; strength and cardio are perfect and effective. The endurance cycling, road, and spin are also favorites.

How has the E2M fitness program changed your life?
E2M fitness is wholistic and I feel like I finally have the tools to keep living a healthy and sustainable lifestyle.

Additional Spice Blends

Buffalo Seasoning

2 teaspoons chili powder
2 teaspoons paprika
1 teaspoon onion powder
1 teaspoon ground garlic
1 teaspoon sea salt
½ teaspoon black pepper
½ teaspoon ground
   cayenne pepper

Greek Seasoning

2 tablespoons dried oregano
1 tablespoon dried dill
1 tablespoon ground garlic
1 tablespoon onion powder
½ teaspoon sea salt
¼ teaspoon black pepper

Adobo Seasoning

1 tablespoon sea salt
1 tablespoon paprika
2 teaspoons black pepper
2 teaspoons ground garlic
1 teaspoon onion powder
1 teaspoon dried oregano
1 teaspoon chili powder
1 teaspoon ground cumin

Veggie Seasoning

3 tablespoons onion powder
1 tablespoon ground garlic
1 tablespoon sea salt
1 teaspoon black pepper
1 teaspoon dried thyme
1 teaspoon paprika
½ teaspoon dried parsley

Curry Powder

4 teaspoons ground coriander
2 teaspoons ground turmeric
2 teaspoons ground mustard
2 teaspoons chili powder
1 teaspoon sea salt
1 teaspoon ground
   cayenne pepper
1 teaspoon ground cumin
½ teaspoon ground cardamom

Garlic and Herb Seasoning

¼ cup sea salt
1 tablespoon ground garlic
1 tablespoon lemon zest
2 teaspoons dried rosemary
1½ teaspoons dried thyme
1½ teaspoons dried oregano
¼ teaspoon paprika
¼ teaspoon crushed
   red pepper

Seafood Spice Blend

1 tablespoon celery seed
1½ teaspoons sea salt
1½ teaspoons sweet paprika
1 teaspoon ground mustard
1 teaspoon ground ginger
5 bay leaves, ground
½ teaspoon smoked paprika
½ teaspoon black pepper
¼ teaspoon crushed red pepper
⅛ teaspoon ground nutmeg
⅛ teaspoon ground cardamom
⅛ teaspoon ground allspice
⅛ teaspoon ground cinnamon
1 pinch of ground cloves

Thai Spice Blend

1¼ tablespoons paprika
2 teaspoons ground turmeric
2 teaspoons black pepper
2 teaspoons ground coriander
2 teaspoons ground fenugreek
2 teaspoons sea salt
1 teaspoon ground mustard
1 teaspoon ground cumin
1 teaspoon ground ginger
¼ teaspoon ground
   cayenne pepper

These scratch-made sauce recipes are a lot easier to make than you may think! They use familiar ingredients you already have on hand, so be sure to stock up! These recipes are packed with loads of flavor. You can finish a dish with these flavorful sauces or use as a marinade for proteins and vegetables.

Just like the salad dressings, a major benefit of homemade sauces is that they are free of preservatives, added sugars, and artificial flavorings. Healthy from the inside out!

Sauces

Sauces

Lemon Herb Tahini Sauce

2 fresh garlic cloves
½ cup fresh lemon juice
½ cup tahini paste
¼ cup water
½ teaspoon sea salt
¼ teaspoon ground cumin
¼ teaspoon dried oregano
1 tablespoon chopped
    fresh parsley

In a food processor, combine the garlic, lemon juice, tahini, water, sea salt, cumin, and oregano; blend until smooth. If the mixture is too thick, add more water to thin it out and adjust the seasoning. Top with parsley.

Spicy Green Schug

2 jalapeños, seeded
    and chopped
¾ cup fresh parsley
¾ cup fresh cilantro
½ cup olive oil
½ cup fresh lemon juice
2 garlic cloves, chopped
½ teaspoon sea salt
¼ teaspoon ground cumin
¼ teaspoon ground coriander

Combine all ingredients in a food processor and blend until thick. Adjust seasoning if needed.

Mango Salsa

1¼ cups diced mango
2 tablespoons lime juice
1 teaspoon chopped
    fresh cilantro
⅛ teaspoon sea salt

Combine all ingredients in a bowl; mix well.

Chimichurri Sauce

¼ cup chopped fresh parsley
¼ cup chopped fresh cilantro
3 garlic cloves, minced
1 tablespoon minced shallots
1 teaspoon seeded and
    minced jalapeño
1 teaspoon dried oregano
¼ teaspoon Dijon mustard
½ cup olive oil
½ cup red wine vinegar
1 teaspoon sea salt
½ teaspoon black pepper

In a food processor, combine the parsley, cilantro, garlic, shallots, jalapeño, oregano, and Dijon mustard. Add the olive oil, red wine vinegar, sea salt, and black pepper. Blend until well combined.

Chipotle Lime Sauce

½ cup lime juice
½ cup olive oil
¼ cup orange juice
¼ cup crushed or chopped
    pineapple (drained)
¼ cup canned chipotle
    pepper (drained)
¼ cup fresh cilantro
2 tablespoons chopped
    green onions
2 tablespoons chopped
    fresh garlic

Combine all ingredients in a food processor and blend until smooth. Adjust seasoning if needed.

Spicy Red Harissa Sauce

1¼ cups canned roasted
    red peppers (drained)
¼ cup olive oil
¼ cup fresh lemon juice
1 tablespoon seeded and
    chopped jalapeño
1 tablespoon chopped
    fresh garlic
1 teaspoon sea salt
¼ teaspoon ground coriander
¼ teaspoon ground cumin
¼ teaspoon chopped fresh mint

Combine all ingredients in a food processor and pulse until the mixture is a thick consistency. Adjust seasoning if needed.

Roasted Garlic Sauce

1 cup olive oil
½ cup garlic cloves
¼ cup water
¼ cup fresh lemon juice
½ teaspoon sea salt
½ teaspoon Dijon mustard
¼ teaspoon black pepper
⅛ teaspoon dried thyme

Preheat the oven to 300 degrees.
   Cover garlic in olive oil and bake in a small oven-safe baking dish for 30 minutes (uncovered). Remove from the oven and cool. Combine the mixture in a food processor with the water, lemon juice, sea salt, Dijon mustard, black pepper, and thyme; blend until smooth.

Sauces

Spicy Peanut Sauce

½ cup peanut butter
¼ cup lime juice
¼ cup water
¼ cup crushed or chopped
   pineapple (drained)
1 tablespoon seeded and
   chopped Fresno chili peppers
1 teaspoon sea salt
1 teaspoon crushed red pepper
½ teaspoon black pepper
¼ teaspoon ground ginger

Combine all ingredients in
a food processor and blend
until smooth. If too thick, add
more water until it is a smooth
consistency. Adjust seasoning
if needed.

Roasted Red Pepper Sauce

1½ cups canned roasted
   red peppers (drained)
¼ cup water
1 tablespoon rice vinegar
1 tablespoon olive oil
1 teaspoon crushed red pepper
¼ teaspoon sea salt
¼ teaspoon black pepper
¼ teaspoon Dijon mustard

Combine all ingredients in
a food processor and blend
until smooth. Adjust seasoning
if needed.

Pineapple and Jalapeño Salsa

1¼ cup diced pineapple
1 tablespoon lime juice
1 teaspoon seeded and
   diced jalapeño
1 teaspoon chopped
   fresh cilantro
⅛ teaspoon sea salt

Combine all ingredients in a
bowl; mix well.

Red Pepper Salsa

1¼ cups seeded and chopped
   red bell peppers
½ cup olive oil
⅓ cup seeded and chopped
   Fresno chili peppers
¼ cup lemon juice
1 tablespoon seeded and
   chopped jalapeño
1 teaspoon sea salt
1 teaspoon chopped fresh garlic
¼ teaspoon ground cumin
¼ teaspoon ground coriander
¼ teaspoon chopped fresh mint

Combine all ingredients in a
food processor and blend until
smooth. Adjust seasoning
if needed.

Tikka Masala Sauce

3 tablespoons olive oil
⅛ teaspoon sesame oil
½ cup diced sweet onions
3½ tablespoons garam
   masala powder
½ cup water
½ cup peanut butter
2 garlic cloves, minced
2 tablespoons lemon juice
1 teaspoon sea salt

Heat the olive oil, sesame oil,
and onions in a sauté pan over
medium-high heat until the
onions start to brown. Add the
garam masala powder; stir and
cook for 30 seconds, and then
add the water. Remove from
the heat.
   Combine the mixture in a
food processor with the peanut
butter, garlic, lemon juice, and
sea salt; blend until smooth.

Spicy Green Harissa

2 cups spinach
½ cup olive oil
½ cup fresh parsley
2 tablespoons seeded
   and diced jalapeño
1 garlic clove
1 tablespoon chopped
   green onions
1 tablespoon ground cumin
1 tablespoon ground coriander
1½ teaspoons sea salt
1 teaspoon smoked paprika
1 teaspoon crushed red pepper

Combine all ingredients in a
food processor and pulse until
the mixture is thick. Adjust
seasoning if needed.

Curry Sauce

3 tablespoons olive oil
⅛ teaspoon sesame oil
½ cup diced sweet onions
3 tablespoons curry powder
½ cup water
½ cup peanut butter
2 garlic cloves, minced
2 tablespoons lemon juice
1 teaspoon sea salt

Heat the olive oil, sesame oil,
and onions in a sauté pan
over medium-high heat. Cook
the onions until they start to
brown. Add the curry powder;
stir and cook for 30 seconds,
and then add the water.
Remove from the heat.
   Combine the mixture in
a food processor with the
peanut butter, garlic cloves,
lemon juice, and sea salt; blend
until smooth.

Meal Planner

Monday
Meal Plan for 4
work days

Tuesday
purchase the
chefs cook books
for yummy
recipes

Wednesday

Thursday

Friday

Saturday

Sunday

Water Tracker

My daily water goal is 1 gallon (128 ounces)

Week (1) 2 3 4 5 6 7 8

Monday

Tuesday

Wednesday

Thursday

Friday

Saturday

Sunday

Week 1 2 3 4 5 6 7 8

Monday

Tuesday

Wednesday

Thursday

Friday

Saturday

Sunday

Water Goals:
How will I reach my water intake goal tomorrow?

Journals & Checklists

E2M Weekly Meal Planner

Grocery List

Veggies

_____

_____

_____

_____

_____

_____

Protein

_____

_____

_____

_____

_____

Other

_____

_____

_____

_____

Monday

Tuesday

Wednesday

Thursday

Friday

Saturday

Sunday

Water Tracker

My daily water goal is 1 gallon (128 ounces).

Week (1) 2 3 4 5 6 7 8

Week 1 2 3 4 5 6 7 8

Monday

Monday

Tuesday

Tuesday

Wednesday

Wednesday

Thursday

Thursday

Friday

Friday

Saturday

Saturday

Sunday

Sunday

Water Goals:

How will I reach my water intake goal tomorrow?

Each glass represents 16 oz.

e2mfitness.com

⅀ Weekly Exercise

Monday	Tuesday

Wednesday	Thursday

Friday	Saturday

Sunday	Non-Scale Victory for the week:
	YAY ME!

Me vs. Me! Trust the Process!

Monthly Habits

Check or color in the square for the new healthy habits you completed.

	Meal Prep	Meal 1	Meal 2	Meal 3	Mindfulness	Workout 1	Workout 2	Jeff's Live	Water Goal	Celebration Meal	Journal
Day 1											
Day 2											
Day 3											
Day 4											
Day 5											
Day 6											
Day 7											
Day 8											
Day 9											
Day 10											
Day 11											
Day 12											
Day 13											
Day 14											
Day 15											
Day 16											
Day 17											
Day 18											
Day 19											
Day 20											
Day 21											
Day 22											
Day 23											
Day 24											
Day 25											
Day 26											
Day 27											
Day 28											
Day 29											
Day 30											
Day 31											

E2M Weekly Meal Planner

Grocery List

Veggies

_____

_____

_____

_____

_____

Protein

_____

_____

_____

_____

_____

Other

_____

_____

_____

_____

Monday

Tuesday

Wednesday

Thursday

Friday

Saturday

Sunday

Water Tracker

My daily water goal is 1 gallon (128 ounces).

Week (1) 2 3 4 5 6 7 8

Monday

Tuesday

Wednesday

Thursday

Friday

Saturday

Sunday

Week 1 2 3 4 5 6 7 8

Monday

Tuesday

Wednesday

Thursday

Friday

Saturday

Sunday

Water Goals:

How will I reach my water intake goal tomorrow?

Each glass represents 16 oz.

e2mfitness.com

⑤M Weekly Exercise

Monday	Tuesday

Wednesday	Thursday

Friday	Saturday

Sunday	Non-Scale Victory for the week:
	YAY ME!

Me vs. Me! Trust the Process!

Monthly Habits

Check or color in the square for the new healthy habits you completed.

	Meal Prep	Meal 1	Meal 2	Meal 3	Mindfulness	Workout 1	Workout 2	Jeff's Live	Water Goal	Celebration Meal	Journal
Day 1											
Day 2											
Day 3											
Day 4											
Day 5											
Day 6											
Day 7											
Day 8											
Day 9											
Day 10											
Day 11											
Day 12											
Day 13											
Day 14											
Day 15											
Day 16											
Day 17											
Day 18											
Day 19											
Day 20											
Day 21											
Day 22											
Day 23											
Day 24											
Day 25											
Day 26											
Day 27											
Day 28											
Day 29											
Day 30											
Day 31											

E2M Weekly Meal Planner

Grocery List

Veggies

_____

_____

_____

_____

_____

Protein

_____

_____

_____

_____

_____

_____

Other

_____

_____

_____

_____

Monday

Tuesday

Wednesday

Thursday

Friday

Saturday

Sunday

Water Tracker

My daily water goal is 1 gallon (128 ounces).

Week ①2 3 4 5 6 7 8

Monday

Tuesday

Wednesday

Thursday

Friday

Saturday

Sunday

Week 1 2 3 4 5 6 7 8

Monday

Tuesday

Wednesday

Thursday

Friday

Saturday

Sunday

Water Goals:

How will I reach my water intake goal tomorrow?

Each glass represents 16 oz.

e2mfitness.com

Weekly Meal Planner

Grocery List

Veggies

_____

_____

_____

_____

_____

_____

Protein

_____

_____

_____

_____

_____

_____

Other

_____

_____

_____

_____

_____

Monday

Tuesday

Wednesday

Thursday

Friday

Saturday

Sunday

Water Tracker

My daily water goal is 1 gallon (128 ounces).

Week ①2 3 4 5 6 7 8

Monday

Tuesday

Wednesday

Thursday

Friday

Saturday

Sunday

Week 1 2 3 4 5 6 7 8

Monday

Tuesday

Wednesday

Thursday

Friday

Saturday

Sunday

Water Goals:

How will I reach my water intake goal tomorrow?

Each glass represents 16 oz.

e2mfitness.com

Made in the USA
Las Vegas, NV
14 December 2023

82779997R00088